TUTANKHAMUN'S TOMB
14th century BCE

TOMB OF PHARAOH SETI I
13th century BCE

HERACLEION
12th century BCE – 8th century CE

ALTAI PRINCESS
5th–3rd century BCE

LIGHTHOUSE OF ALEXANDRIA
4th century BCE – 14th century CE

BUST OF NEFERTITI
14th century BCE

TENEA
12th century BCE – 6th century CE

POMPEII
6th century BCE – 1st century CE

ANCIENT EGYPTIAN BARIS SHIP
5th century BCE

4th century BCE

FAMOUS FINDS AND FINDERS

SEARCHING FOR THE PAST

Albatros

SEEKERS OF THE PAST

When people hear the word *archeology*, many think of Steven Spielberg's movies about brave adventurers or a sci-fi theme park with dinosaurs. But the way popular movies portray archeology doesn't match up with reality. As for the second movie, we can safely say that no paleontologists spend their time running from predatory *Tyrannosaurus rexes*. Instead, they search for fossilized fragments that have been buried in the ground for hundreds of millions of years, often several dozen feet apart, before taking their discoveries to a lab, where state-of-the-art technology creates images of past giants. Successful paleontologists add to the puzzle that helps us understand life on our planet.

SUE HENDRICKSON – SUE THE *T. REX*

Paleontologists study long-extinct animal and plant life. Archeologists study anything related to human history. Where these two disciplines meet, we find two discoveries that help shape our understanding of human evolution. These are Misses Ardi and Lucy, whose remains give us a better idea of what Australopithecus and Ardipithecus, our most distant ancestors, were like. Sometimes, a non-archeologist might stumble upon an ancient ancestor while hiking in the mountains. This happened to Erica and Helmut, the discoverers of Ötzi the iceman.

DONALD JOHANSON WITH LUCY

YOSHITSUGU KOBAYASHI,
PROFESSOR AT HOKKAIDO UNIVERSITY (LEFT)

YOHANNES HAILE-SELASSIE WITH MISS ARDI

FAMOUS FINDERS

One day, our cities will disappear and new ones will be built in their place. Future generations will think of us as ancestors. The people who discover the ruins of these cities may become as famous as 19th-century travelers who, determined to find lost human civilizations, uncovered cities that were drowned, buried under lava from volcanic eruptions, or destroyed in mythical battles. Legends about these cities guided the explorers in their quest. Archeologists in labs are the key to unlocking the mysteries of these cities, allowing us to simulate time travel.

EXPLORING THE LASCAUX CAVE

DOMENICO FONTANA: POMPEII

HEINRICH SCHLIEMANN: TROY

JOHN L. STEPHENS: CHICHEN ITZA

ROBERT KOLDEWEY: BABYLON

UNKNOWN FINDERS

The ruins of old cities and found objects tell us not only how people lived, but also how they perceived the world around them. Frescoes on the walls of ancient dwellings and cave paintings tell us about the first human homes. By studying the *Venus de Milo*, we learn how Ancient Greece sculptors perceived beauty, while looking at the *Venus of Dolní Věstonice* may tell us how prehistoric women saw themselves. Anthropologists, who study humans, look for parallels between the past and present, which is why some finds are associated with a scientist rather than the person who discovered them. For example, leading Czech archeologist Karel Absolon is associated with the *Venus of Dolní Věstonice*, although a layman found the figurine by chance. A peasant discovered the *Venus de Milo*. Four teenage boys in France discovered the cave paintings in Lascaux Cave, and Maria, the daughter of archeologist Marcelino Sanz de Sautuola, discovered the cave paintings in the Cave of Altamira in Spain.

MARIA SANZ DE SAUTUOLA: ALTAMIRA

MARCELINO SANZ DE SAUTUOLA: ALTAMIRA

ELENA KORKA: TENEA

WHO WRITES HISTORY?

Even when the finder is an archeologist, some finds are not attributed to them. Universities and museums tend to claim interesting finds for themselves. The general public learned the names of the archeologists who made the Sutton Hoo discovery relatively recently, thanks to a film adaptation of the story. The film shows the events surrounding the discovery of the tomb of an Anglo-Saxon king, which made history shortly before World War II, when history was being written for a different reason.

SUTTON HOO

APPARENTLY UNREMARKABLE FINDINGS

Not only can people change our ideas on the workings of the past, but an ordinary-looking piece of stone can do it too. The Rosetta Stone is a stele that has taught us a lot about hieroglyphics. Like many simple pot fragments, its discovery caused many scientists to revise their theories.

ROSETTA STONE

TIME UNDER THE SURFACE

Those who want to dig up treasures with a pickaxe and shovel must be ready to work hard. Because of this, archeologists need the help of laborers. Fragments of the past are buried not only in the ground, but also on the beds of rivers, seas, and oceans. The cradle of life is also the tomb of many water-going vessels.

KARLSRUHE

ANDERS FRANZÉN:
THE *VASA*

BARRY CLIFFORD:
THE *WHYDAH GALLEY*

ROBERT BALLARD:
THE *TITANIC*

FRANCK GODDIO:
HERACLEION

ALVIN – THE *TITANIC*

MODERN TECHNOLOGY

Modern technology comes into play, allowing oceanographers to go deeper and deeper into the ocean—some in just a pressure suit, others in a research submarine. These submarines are designed to allow the crew to descend as deep as possible. When the crew can't reach a certain depth, a remote-controlled submarine can. This way, explorers can uncover the mysteries of the abyss without getting their feet wet.

BURIED RULERS

In swallowing what it finds, the ocean doesn't distinguish between ancient and recent. Luxury oceangoing liners and warships alike have gone below the surface for an involuntary rest, only to re-emerge thanks to scientific advances in their future. It's like they are rulers of great empires, woken from a long sleep by a time ahead of their own. In 2022, we celebrated the 100th anniversary of Howard Carter's discovery of Tutankhamen's tomb and the extravagant riches the pharaoh took to the Afterlife. So the present forever becomes the past, which our yet-unborn descendants will learn about. Hopefully, we won't do anything to shame ourselves. If we do, the Future will surely find out.

HOWARD CARTER: TUTANKHAMUN

DISCOVERY OF THE OSEBERG SHIP

ÖTZI

(œtsi)

DISCOVERED BY:
German tourists Helmut and Erika Simon

THE VERY FIRST MUMMY FROM THE LATE STONE AGE FOUND IN A STATE OF PERFECT PRESERVATION – WITH INTERNAL ORGANS, REMNANTS OF CLOTHING, AND TOOLS

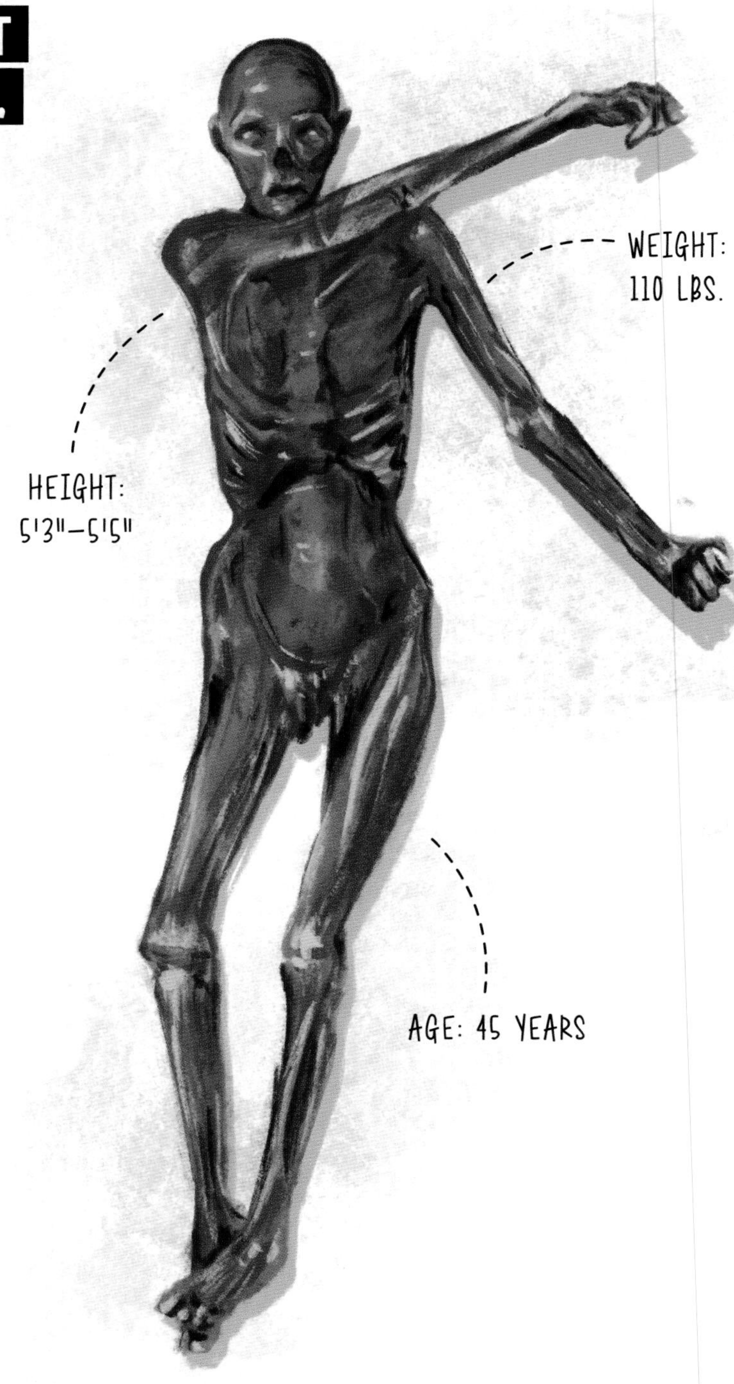

A BODY IN THE ICE

The Simons thought they had found the remains of a recently lost climber—until scientists at the University of Innsbruck revealed that the corpse was over 3,000 years old.

WHO WAS ÖTZI?

At 45 years old, prehistoric Ötzi was considered old for his time. He was muscular, sinewy, and physically fit, even though he was sick. Ötzi had pain in his back, knees, and ankles, and he also had gum disease, tooth decay, and constriction of the arteries. Since he couldn't digest lactose, he couldn't drink milk or eat dairy products.

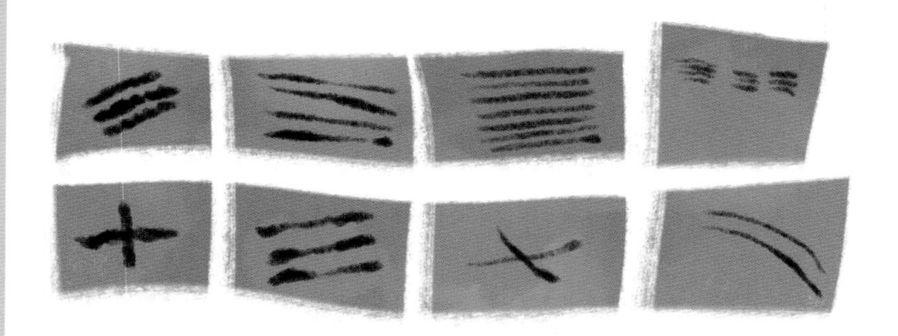

61 TATTOOS

The 61 tattooed symbols on Ötzi's body show that our ancestor tried to cure his ailments. These marks aren't for decoration; they're healer's symbols made of crushed charcoal, intended to alleviate Ötzi's pain.

ÖTZI'S END

Although Ötzi was very sick, he didn't die of natural causes. He bled to death after being hit by an arrow from behind, as shown by a wound below his left shoulder. Examination showed that his last meal was ibex meat and wheat cakes. We'll likely never know who killed Ötzi or why.

WHERE:
Austria, Ötz Valley
WHEN:
1991
ÖTZ VALLEY
POUCH SIMILAR TO TODAY'S FANNY PACK, IN WHICH ÖTZI KEPT A SCRAPER, A DRILL, A BLADE, FEATHERS FOR HIS ARROWS, AND TINDER
BACKPACK REINFORCED WITH HAZEL RODS AND A WOODEN BOARD
BEARSKIN HAT
COPPER AXE WITH YEW SHAFT – IN ÖTZI'S TIME, A GREAT RARITY
CLOAK WOVEN FROM A COMBINATION OF GRASS AND SHEEP AND GOATSKIN
VESSEL MADE OF BIRCH BARK
SHOES OF GOATSKIN STUFFED WITH HAY, WITH BEARSKIN SOLES AND COWHIDE LACES. REMARKABLY, THEIR PROPERTIES COULD COMPETE WITH THOSE OF ULTRAMODERN TREKKING SHOES.

LUCY

(lu:si)

WHERE:	WHEN:
Ethiopia, Hadar	1974

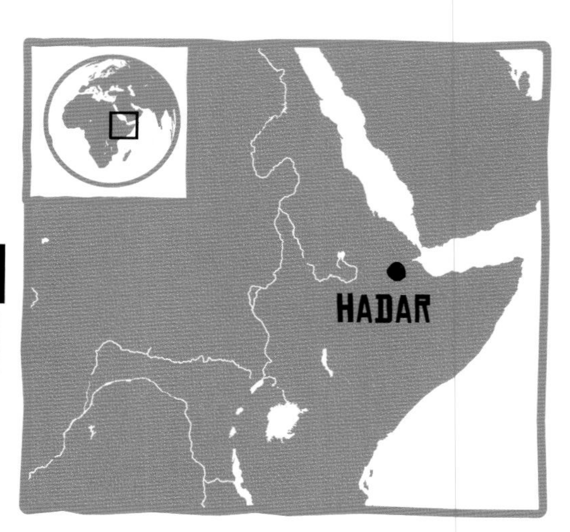

WITH THE DISCOVERY OF THIS PARTIALLY PRESERVED SKELETON OF AUSTRALOPITHECUS AFARENSIS, SCIENTISTS WERE ABLE TO DETERMINE THE APPEARANCE AND WAY OF LIFE OF AN AUSTRALOPITHECINE SPECIES, REVEALING MORE ABOUT THE ORIGINS OF MAN.

WHOSE ARM IS THIS?

In November 1974, paleoanthropologist Donald Johanson of the University of Cleveland was exploring the valley of the Awash River when he came across a fragment of an arm bone protruding from the slope. To everyone's amazement, it turned out to belong not to an ape but to a hominid—a precursor of humans. In three weeks of intensive work, Professor Johanson and his team assembled 40 percent of the skeleton. This skeleton is almost 3.18 million years old . . .

HEIGHT: APPROX. 3'7"

WEIGHT: APPROX. 62 LBS.

THE BEATLES

LUCY IN THE SKY . . .

Based on the pelvic bone found, scientists determined that the subject was a woman of an australopithecine species. Since one of the team's favorite songs was "Lucy in the Sky with Diamonds" by the Beatles, it didn't take them long to come up with the nickname "Lucy."

FOUR STAGES PRECEDING CONTEMPORARY MAN

AUSTRALOPITHECUS AFARENSIS	HOMO HABILIS	HOMO ERECTUS	HOMO NEANDERTHALENSIS

DISCOVERED BY:
paleoanthropologist Donald Johanson

A MYSTERIOUS DEATH

Lucy was probably 12 when she died. Why did she die so young? In 2016, a group of experts came up with the theory that she sustained injuries in a fall from a tall tree, including fractures to the shoulder joints and arms, and therefore probably had severe damage to the internal organs. Other scientists, including Lucy's discoverers, believe that she was killed by an animal that then stamped on her body.

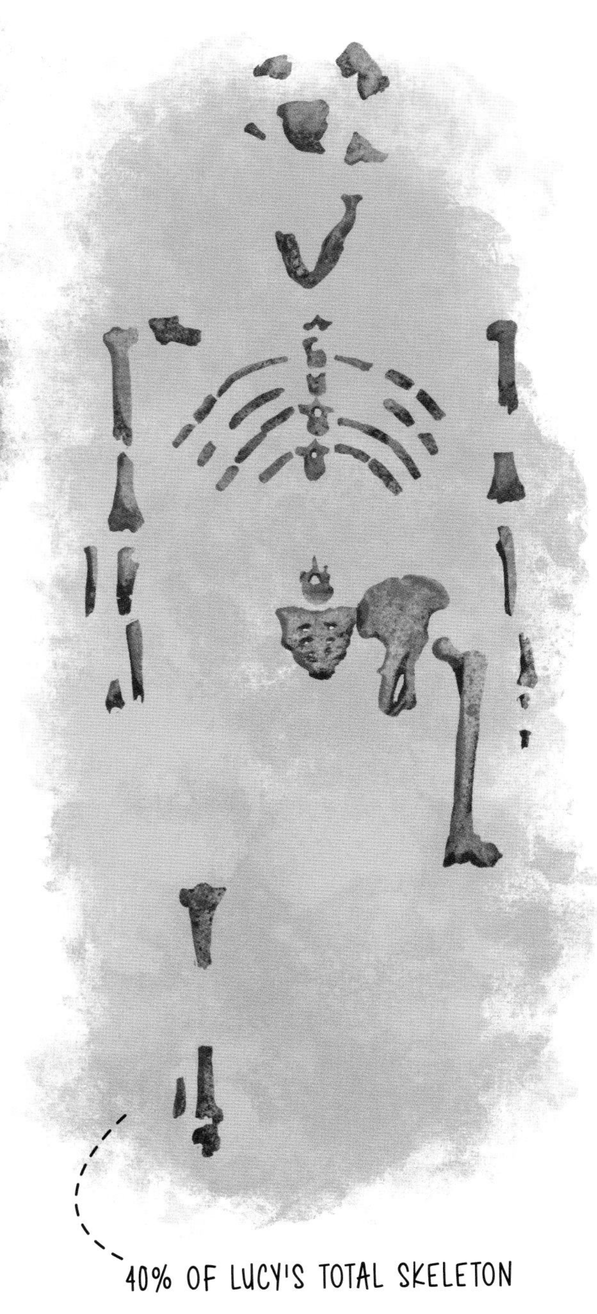

WHAT WAS FOR LUNCH?

The basic diet of australopithecines comprised sedges, grass, leaves, and fruit, and also some meat. These hominids made and used the first stone tools.

ON ALL FOURS OR UPRIGHT?

Thanks to Lucy, we know that our australopithecine ancestors walked upright on two legs, like us. Unlike us, though, they were such agile climbers that they could live in the trees. Since females were considerably smaller and more vulnerable than males, they were more likely to find safety in high branches.

DISCOVERED BY:
Yohannes Haile-Selassie

MISS ARDI

Ardi (ʌrdi)

REMAINS OF ARDIPITHECUS RAMIDUS [KNOWN AS ARDI], AN EARLY HOMINID ANCESTOR, WHO LIVED BETWEEN 4.4 MILLION AND 6 MILLION YEARS AGO.

A LONG WAIT

Since 1992, archeologists have been finding remains of our ancestors in Ethiopia. It was there that the first remains of Miss Ardi were discovered in 1994. After that, experts gradually succeeded in compiling an almost-entire skeleton of an *Ardipithecus ramidus* female. The complete results of many years of research were published in 2009.

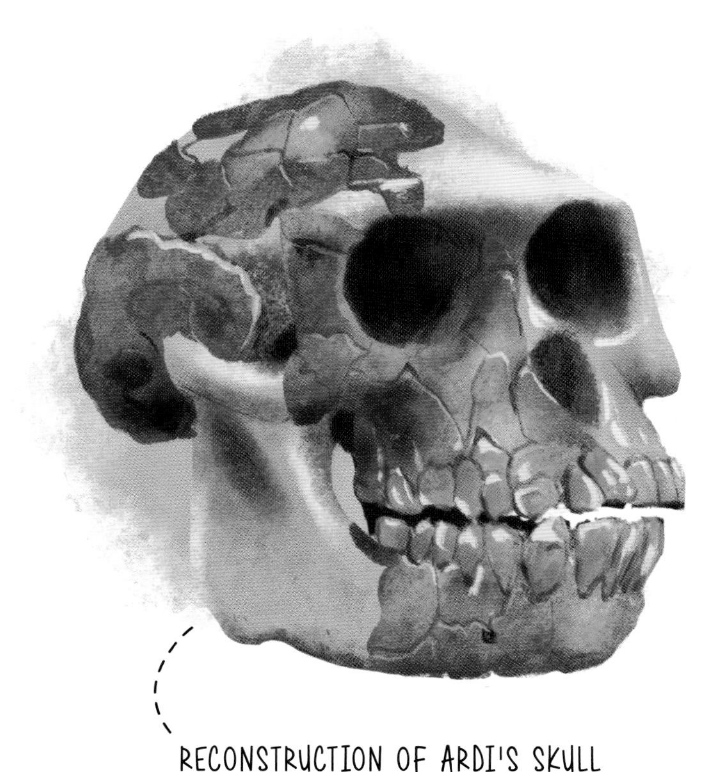

RECONSTRUCTION OF ARDI'S SKULL

NEITHER CHIMP NOR HUMAN

Miss Ardi was neither chimpanzee nor human. The build of her limbs testifies that she walked upright on two legs, although she sometimes leaned forward on clenched fists. Ardi was an excellent climber who could jump from branch to branch with ease.

WHY IS ARDI SO IMPORTANT?

The discovery of Miss Ardi and her relations gives us some idea of how humankind evolved from an ancestor we share with the chimpanzee, although scientists have yet to discover specifics about this common ancestor. It seems, however, that it was 2 million years older than *Ardipithecus ramidus*.

WHERE: Ethiopia, Hadar

WHEN: 1992

ARDI'S DIET

Like Lucy and her kind, Ardi and others of the species *Ardipithecus ramidus* lived on plants, fungus, leaves, nuts, and the flesh of small animals. In the procurement of food, they used only twigs and unworked stones (things that were at hand) and not tools.

CHINCHORRO MUMMIES

Chinchorro (tʃin-tʃo-ro)

PROBABLY THE OLDEST MUMMIES IN THE WORLD ARE THE 200 SUCH BODIES OF MEMBERS OF THE CHINCHORRO CULTURE.

WHO WERE THE PEOPLE OF THE CHINCHORRO CULTURE?

People of the Chinchorro culture of South America lived on the coast of Chile between 7000 BCE and 1500 BCE. As well as being experienced fishermen, they were skilled weavers of mats and wicker objects and lived in a highly egalitarian society. Therefore, we know that the mummified bodies are not the remains of high-status individuals. They represent a cross-section of society composed of men, women, and children.

AND FIRST PLACE GOES TO . . . CHINCHORRO

When we hear the words *mummy* and *mummification*, our first thoughts are of Ancient Egypt. Yet the Chinchorro mummies originated a full 2,000 years earlier than the first Egyptian ones.

WHERE:
Chile,
Camarones
Valley

WHEN:
1914

DISCOVERED BY:
German archeologist Max Uhle

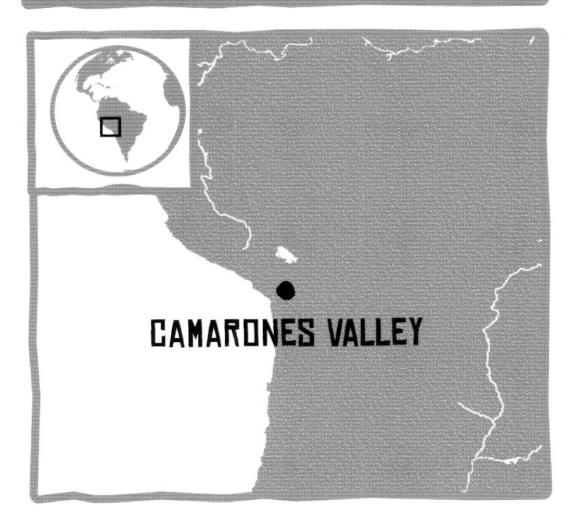

BLACK MUMMIES

Scientists have learned that the oldest of the Chinchorro mummies—known as the "black mummies" due to the paint used—originated between 5050 BCE and 3000 BCE. The mummifiers plainly knew what they were doing. First, they removed all skin, soft tissue, and internal organs from the body. Then they filled the body cavity with a wooden construction, reeds, and dried herbs. After that, they refitted the skin to the body and painted it black. They covered the face with a clay mask and set a short black wig on the head.

RED MUMMIES

Around 2500 BCE, the mummification process had become simpler. The result was the so-called "red mummy." Now it was enough for the mummifier to remove all organs and soft tissue from the abdomen and head, pack the body with various materials including clay, set a wig of long human hair on the head, and paint everything with red ochre. They decorated the body, including the face, with red clay.

WHY MUMMIFY?

In ancient times, mummification had a deep religious significance. The preservation of the body not only honored the dead but also ensured their afterlife in the next world.

WHERE:
Russia,
Ukok Plateau, Altai
Mountains, Siberia

WHEN:
1993

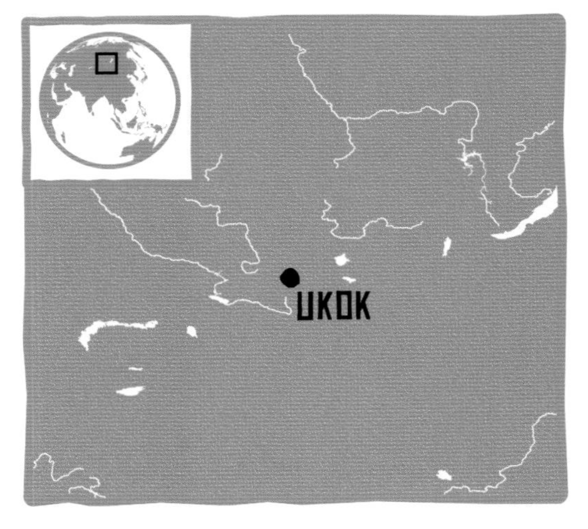

ALTAI PRINCESS

Altai (altaj/)

MUMMY OF A YOUNG WOMAN OF THE ALTAI PEOPLE, ON WHOSE SKIN IS PRESERVED ONE OF THE WORLD'S FIRST AND MOST BEAUTIFUL TATTOOS.

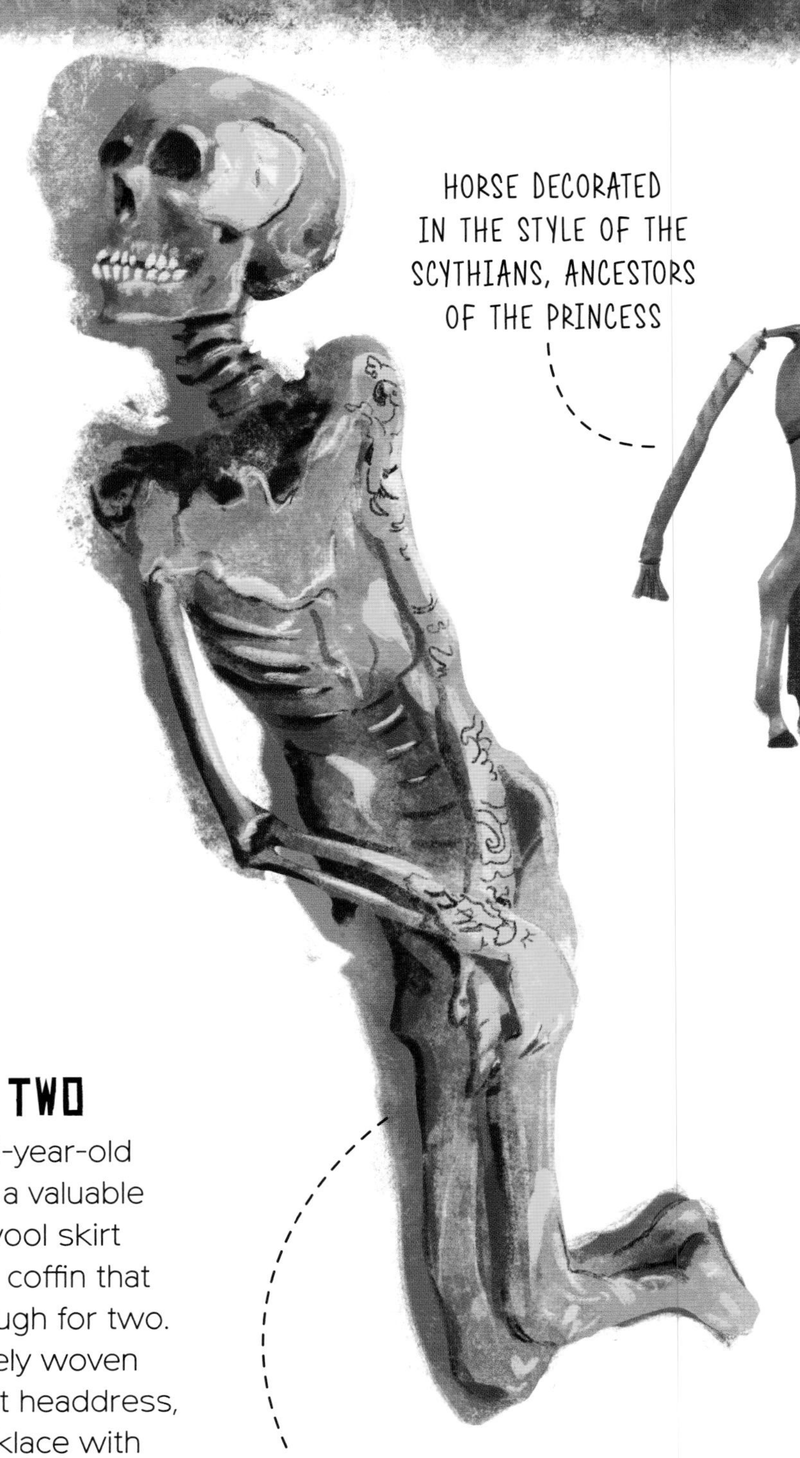

HORSE DECORATED IN THE STYLE OF THE SCYTHIANS, ANCESTORS OF THE PRINCESS

ANCIENT PEOPLE OF THE PAZYRYK CULTURE

In 1993, Natalia Polosmak went to Siberia convinced that she would discover the graves of the nomadic Pazyryk people of the Iron Age. She was right. The grave she discovered belonged to a prominent member of this nation who is now known as the Altai Princess.

A COFFIN FOR TWO

The mummy of a 25-year-old woman dressed in a valuable silk blouse and a wool skirt lay in a larch-wood coffin that was easily big enough for two. She had an intricately woven hairstyle, a large felt headdress, and a wooden necklace with gold-covered ornaments.

THE MUMMY WAS DISCOVERED INTACT

DISCOVERED BY:
Russian scientist Natalia Polosmak

AN ENVIABLE TATTOO

Another unique feature of the "Siberian Princess" was her superbly drawn and magnificently well-preserved tattoo. Her left shoulder was adorned with a scene containing a deer with the beak of an eagle, the horns of a goat, and the heads of griffins (lions with an eagle's head and wings). We do not know whether the purpose of the tattoo was religious, curative, or ritualistic. One thing is for sure, though: the woman died at age 25 from breast cancer, which she had suffered from for three years.

TATTOO FORM

PRINCESS OR PRIESTESS?

The rare larch-wood coffin, the beautiful jewels, the apparel, and the remains of six sacrificial horses make it clear that this woman was of high social status. It is likely that she was a Pazyryk priestess.

PERIOD REPRESENTATION OF THE MYTHICAL MINOTAUR

FRESCO PORTRAYING A JUMP OVER A BULL

LABYRINTH FROM MYTHOLOGY

As the seat of Minoan rulers, the palace at Knossos represented the Minoan culture of Ancient Crete, which is known for its cult of the bull. The palace's extremely intricate, maze-like interior begs the question as to whether it really did house the mythical Minotaur, a monster with a human body and a bull's head.

ONCE UPON A TIME . . .

Minoan culture has been around since the Bronze Age (2700–1450 BCE). The greatest time for Minoan expansion was 2000–1600 BCE, when Knossos had a population of about 18,000. Knossos was later abandoned for reasons that remain unclear. It could have been because of a volcanic eruption on Santorini or an attack from the Mycenaeans of the Greek interior.

THE PALACE COVERED AN AREA OF NEARLY 4 ACRES.

TENEA

(t̪ɛːneä)

DISCOVERED BY:
Peloponnese villagers; archeologist Elena Korka

THE UNCOVERING OF ITS RUINS PROVED THE EXISTENCE OF THIS CITY KNOWN FROM MYTHOLOGY.

A CHANCE DISCOVERY

In 1984, people in the village of Chiliomodi were digging a canal when they found something unusual. It turned out to be an ancient sarcophagus. Believing they had a historical treasure, they contacted Elena Korka, a young Greek archeologist. But at the time, Korka didn't have enough experience to work on such an important find and had to wait for her chance.

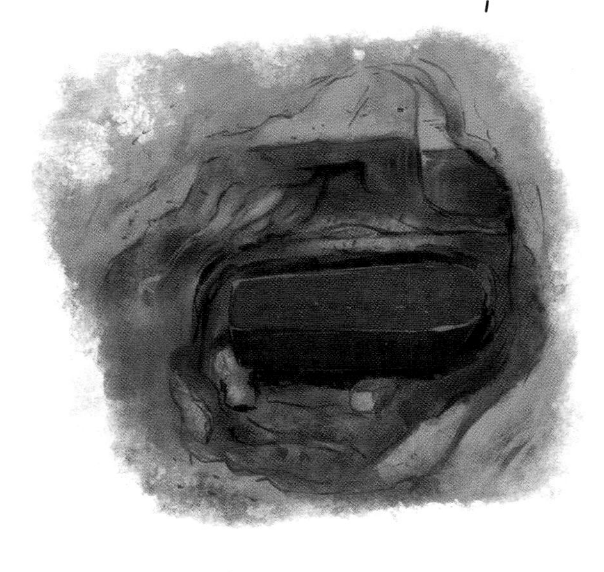

AT LAST!

By 2013, when Elena Korka returned to the Peloponnese region, she was a very experienced archeologist. Soon, her team had uncovered 40 sarcophagi, ruins of well-constructed walls, stone and marble floors, remains of houses, oil lamps Ⓐ, about 200 coins Ⓑ (one made specifically for the journey to the afterlife), and seven graves containing items like precious vases Ⓒ and jewels Ⓓ. Everything found so far here is clear proof of the ancient city's great wealth and fame.

REMAINS CONTAINED IN A SARCOPHAGUS

WHERE:
Greece, Peloponnese region

WHEN:
1984 and 2013

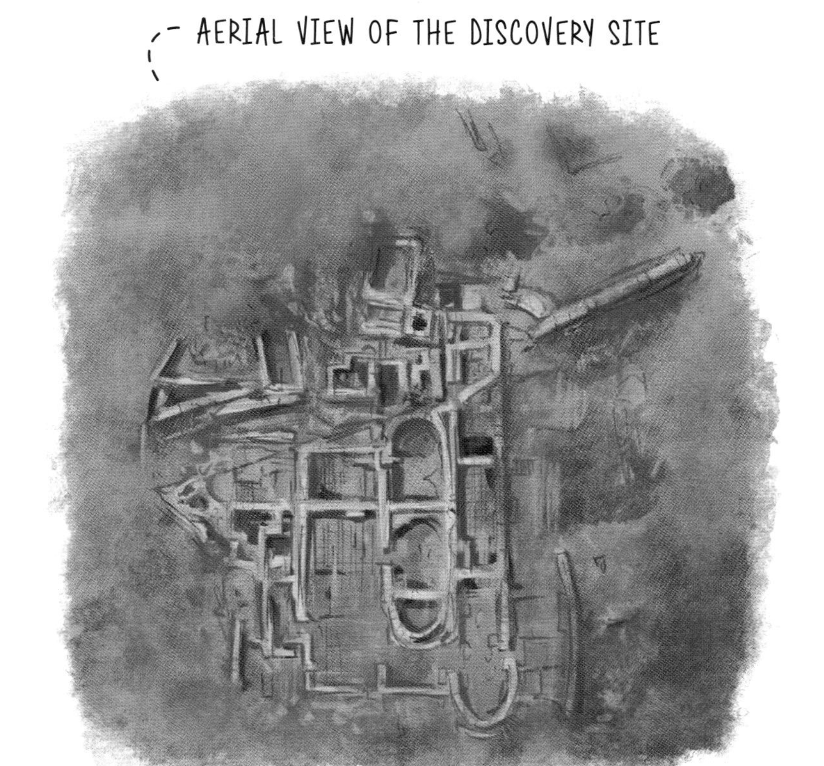

A FAMOUS CITY

Legend has it, Tenea was founded in 1100 BCE by Trojan prisoners of war who had been defeated in the Trojan War. The new city was built on an important road between Corinth and Mycenae, not by accident. Legend also says that Oedipus, son of King Laius of Thebes, grew up in Tenea, one of the biggest and most successful ancient cities.

GLORIOUS TENEA'S END

Tenea was successful for many years, especially under Roman emperor Septimius Severus (193–211 CE). Later, in the 4th century CE, barbarian Gothic tribes attacked the Peloponnese region, causing a lot of damage. We believe that the city was abandoned for good in the 6th century.

CHICHEN ITZA

(tʃiˈtʃen itˈsa)

WHERE: Mexico, Yucatan

WHEN: 1841

ONE OF THE BEST-PRESERVED CITIES OF THE MAYAN CIVILIZATION

IN THE FOOTSTEPS OF THE MAYA

Since John Lloyd Stephens was an adventurer at heart, no one was surprised by his eagerness to find the legendary Mayan civilization. In the 1840s, Stephens and his artist friend Frederick Catherwood went to Mexico with this goal in mind. They visited 44 Mayan cities and discovered Chichen Itza.

I WANT TO GO TO CHICHEN ITZA TOO!

As soon as a Mayan city was found in the Yucatan jungle, archeologists rushed to explore it, making the site one of Mexico's most important archeological zones.

DISCOVERED BY:
American writer and adventurer John Lloyd Stephens

IMPORTANT PLACES

The foot of the pyramid is decorated with the head of the serpent god Kukulcán Ⓐ. In certain light, the steps have a zigzagging shadow in the shape of a serpent. The complex had its own observatory Ⓑ where priests studied the night sky. The city's inhabitants played a game called pok-ta-pok on a special court Ⓒ. One of the city's monuments has 200 columns Ⓓ.

WHAT WE KNOW ABOUT CHICHEN ITZA

The Mayan city Chichen Itza was founded in the 5th century CE at a place that had been an important pilgrimage site for thousands of years. During the period from 600–800 CE, the city's golden age, it developed into a thriving social, political, spiritual, and commercial center. It is believed that the city was abandoned practically overnight. No one knows why.

A PYRAMID AND A PLUMED SERPENT

El Castillo is the name of a pyramid at Chichen Itza. Twice a year, an important Mayan god appears there in the form of a plumed serpent. Although the spectacle is caused only by a play of light and shadow during the spring and autumn equinoxes, it illustrated the Mayan belief that their mighty god was descending the pyramid from its tip to the ground in the form of a large plumed serpent.

HERACLEION

(hɛɹəkljən)

DISCOVERED BY:
French archeologist
Franck Goddio

THE REDISCOVERED ANCIENT CITY IS IN A PERFECT STATE OF PRESERVATION, MAKING IT AN IMPORTANT RESOURCE FOR RESEARCH INTO HOW ITS PEOPLE LIVED.

BEHOLD A SHIP! BUT IT'S A DIFFERENT ONE!

In 2000, underwater archeologist Franck Goddio and his team plunged into the Nile River hoping to retrieve a lost 18th-century warship from the deep. They found a ship—but it was considerably older, from Ancient Egypt. And that wasn't all: under a thick layer of silt, the explorers discovered the lost ancient city of Heracleion, also known as Thonis, in addition to 64 ships.

GLORY DAYS OF HERACLEION

This important Egyptian port city, which spread across four islands, originated in the 12th century BCE. Glory and extraordinary wealth arrived quickly. In its heyday, Heracleion was a place of trade with the Greeks and a collection point for taxes and customs duties, and it was regarded as the most important port on the Mediterranean. Over time, however, the city's fame waned. Then, in the 2nd century BCE, an earthquake struck and sent it down into the waves. Yet the city was never forgotten.

WHERE:
Egypt,
Nile Delta

WHEN:
2000

RICHES UPON RICHES

From the start, Franck Goddio's discoveries showed how wealthy the city was. They included 13-foot-tall statues of gods, a temple dedicated to the god Amun, tons of coins, and valuable objects like stone slabs with Greek and Egyptian inscriptions that told stories about the everyday lives of Heracleion's residents.

PORT ROYAL

WHERE:
Jamaica,
Caribbean Sea

WHEN:
1981–1991

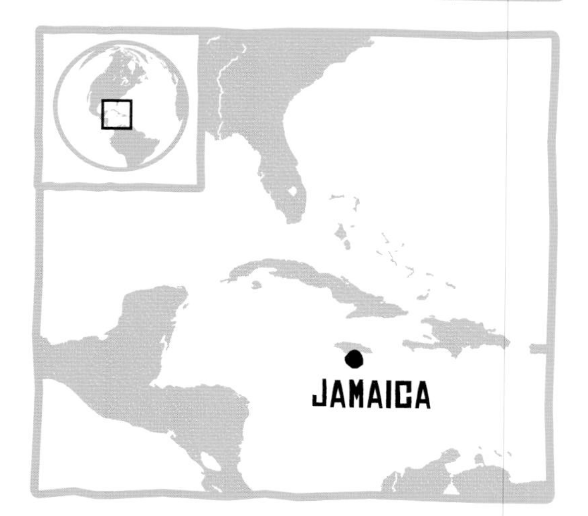

RUINS OF A JAMAICAN PORT TOWN THAT SERVED AS A REFUGE FOR PIRATES IN THE 17TH CENTURY. IT WAS DESTROYED BY AN EARTHQUAKE.

HUGE WAVES! HELP!

On June 7, 1692, the Caribbean coast was hit by a huge earthquake followed by a massive tsunami that destroyed everything in its path, including the wealthy port town of Port Royal, Jamaica's unofficial capital. In a single sweep, the wave wiped out brick houses, stone streets, and the 3,000 people of Port Royal.

DISCOVERED BY:
a team of archeologists from the University of Texas

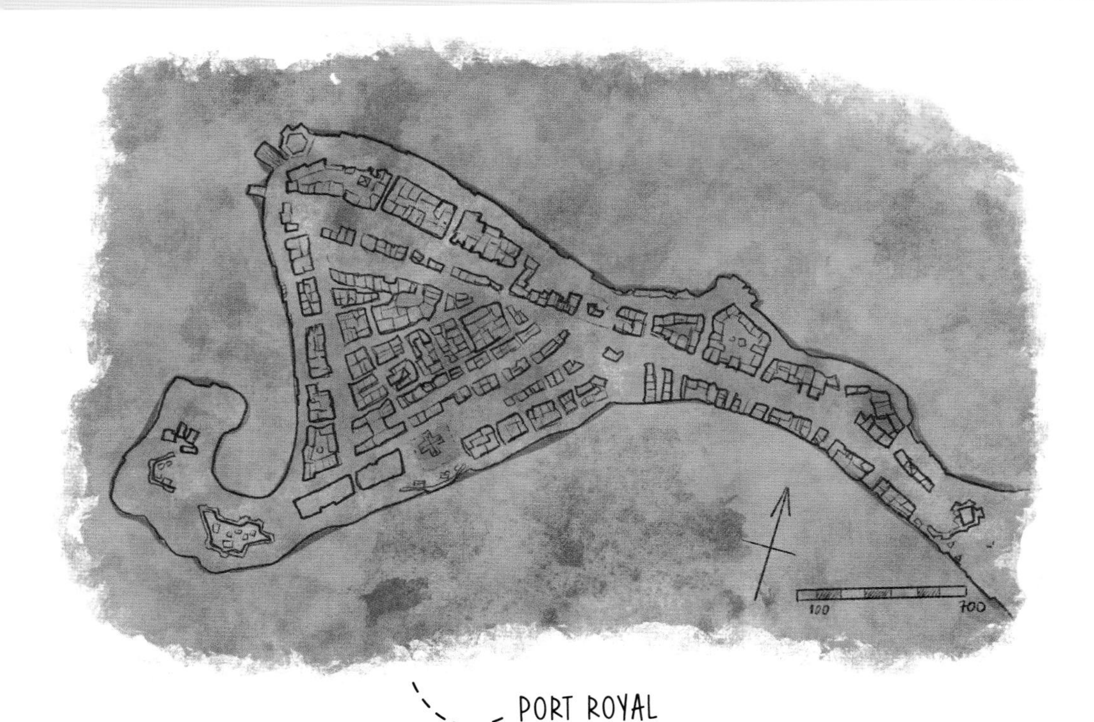

PORT ROYAL

PROPER HOUSES

News of a pirate paradise in Jamaica spread fast, and undesirable people rushed to Port Royal. To accommodate the newcomers, the English governor ordered new brick houses be built. To save space, these houses were tall—a mistake in an earthquake-prone region. Earlier inhabitants of the town had only built lightweight wooden houses.

DIVINE RETRIBUTION

Believers in divine retribution must have been thrilled when this town was wiped off the face of the earth, as it was known for its sin and vice. This is unsurprising because the only people living there were brutal pirates, buccaneers, and convicts, and there was a bar or inn on every corner.

DREADED PIRATE LEADER BLACKBEARD (1680–1718)

HENRY MORGAN, ONE OF THE BEST KNOWN PIRATE LEADERS (1635–1688)

PIRATES ON DUTY

Until 1655, Jamaica was inhabited by the native Taino people and peaceful Spanish sugar cane farmers. But everything changed when the English took control of the island, occupied the town, and filled it with stone houses and shops. They then invited the Brethren of the Coast, a group of pirates and buccaneers, to defend Jamaica from the Spanish.

RICHES AT THE BOTTOM OF THE SEA

Between 1981 and 1991, a team of scientists from Texas A&M University conducted diving expeditions to the bottom of the Caribbean to figure out the mysteries of the sunken pirate town of Port Royal and how its people had lived. In addition to bulwarks and ruined houses, they found dozens of wrecked ships that had once belonged to pirates or honest merchants, along with many valuable goods. Among the treasures was a watch that had stopped at 11:43 on June 7, 1692, the moment when the destruction of Port Royal, the "sinners' town," began.

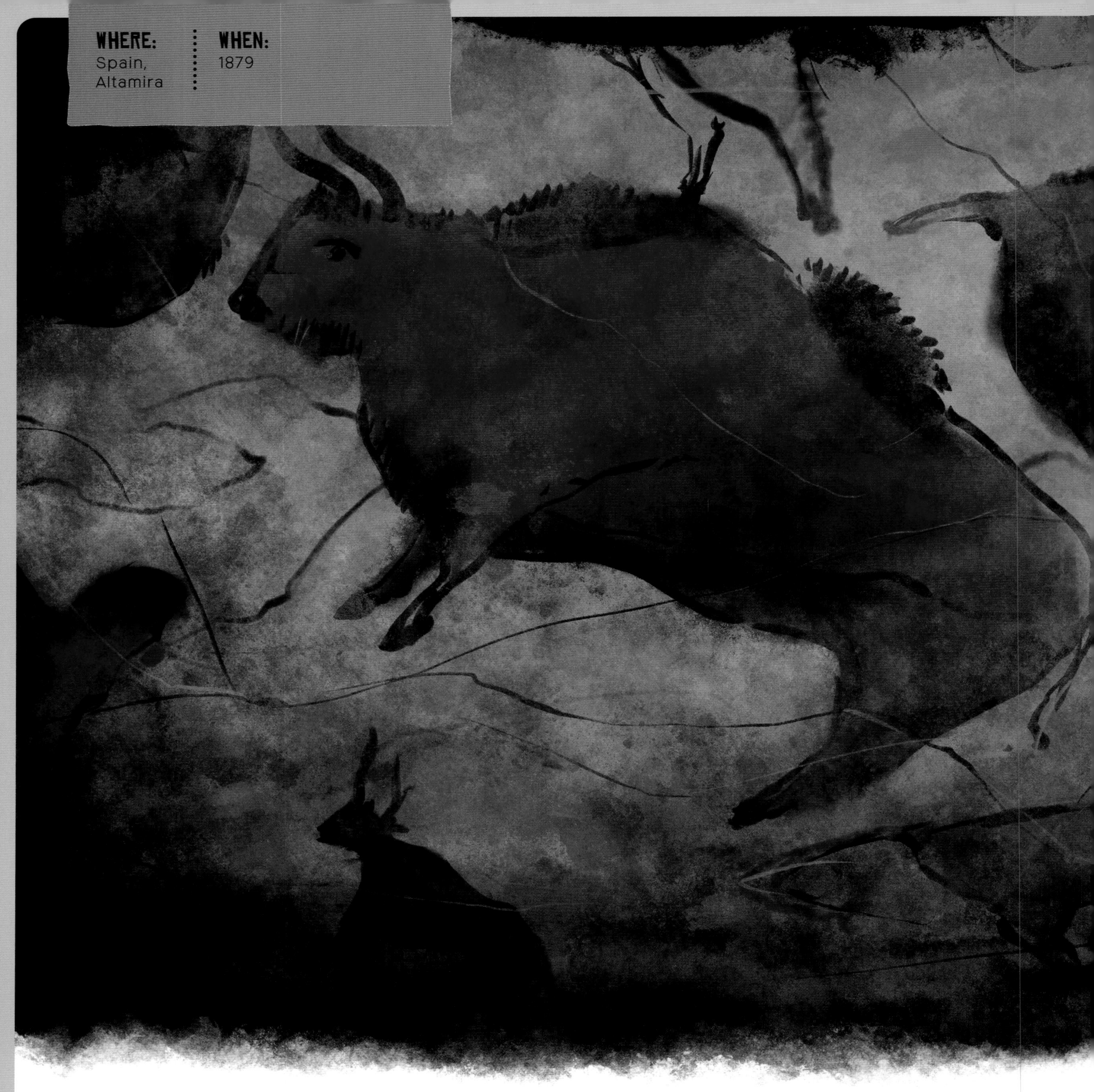

WHERE: Spain, Altamira

WHEN: 1879

ALTAMIRA

(æltəˈmɪərə)

FIRST DISCOVERY OF CAVE PAINTINGS WITH A PREHISTORIC ORIGIN.

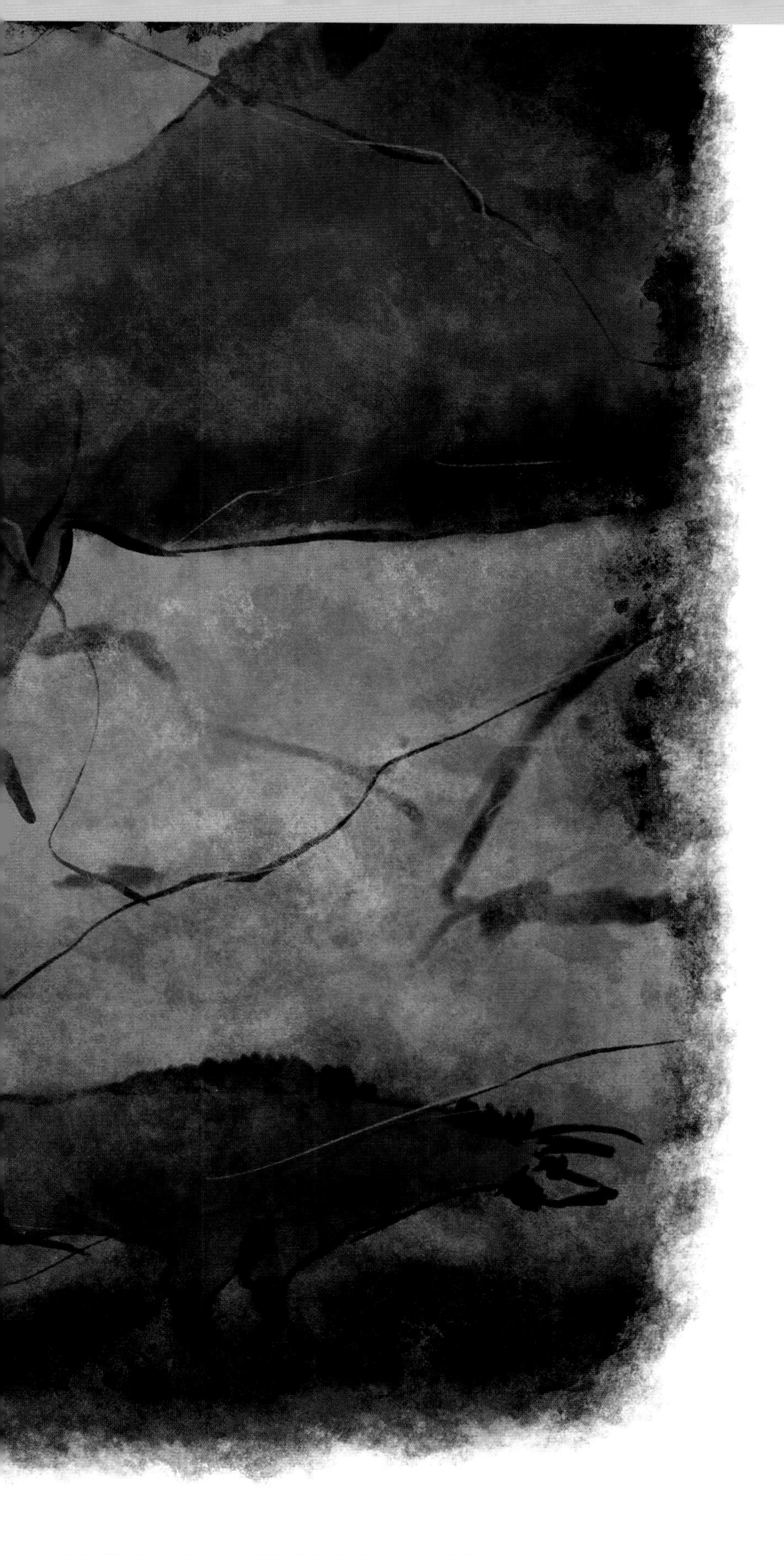

DISCOVERED BY:
Maria, five-year-old daughter of amateur archeologist Marcelino Sanz de Sautuola

THERE ARE BULLS HERE, DAD!

Marcelino Sanz de Sautuola was an amateur archeologist who, in 1879, along with his daughter Maria, set out to explore a cave he owned. Marcelino found flint tools and animal bones, while Maria went deeper into the cave and called out, "Daddy! Daddy! Bulls!" Marcelino rushed over and saw a cave wall covered with beautiful prehistoric paintings.

PREHISTORIC HERD AND MORE

The wall clearly showed a herd of bison and some prehistoric horses, deer, and wild boars, each accurately depicted in red, brown, and black. The paintings dated back to 15,000–10,000 BCE. Little Maria didn't seem to notice that there wasn't a single bull among them.

HEY DOGGIE? HERE, BOY!

It was 1868, and Spanish hunter Modesto Cubillas and his dog were out hunting when the dog disappeared into some kind of crevice. "Hey doggie? Here boy!" Modesto called before climbing into the space himself. At the end of it, he didn't find his dog, but a cave. He quickly reported his discovery to Marcelino Sanz de Sautuola, the landowner.

MAGDALENIAN STYLE

The paintings in the Cave of Altamira are known for their Magdalenian style. These painters liked to depict their animal subjects with lots of detail, including fur, trunks, horns, hooves, and manes. The figures are realistically proportioned and shown in expressive attitudes. Before the Magdalenian style, there was the Périgord style (30,000–13,000 BCE), which was characterized by twisted perspective, sprayed paintwork, animals depicted in profile but with horns shown from the front, and simple representation.

LASCAUX

(læsˈkoʊ)

CAVE COMPLEX DUBBED THE "SISTINE CHAPEL OF PREHISTORY" FOR ITS MANY WALL PAINTINGS, DISCOVERED BY FOUR BOYS LOOKING FOR TREASURE

A FAIRYTALE TREASURE

According to local legend, just beyond the village of Montignac lay a tunnel containing fairytale proportions of treasures. In 1940, four teenagers were fascinated by a hole in the ground, and to see how deep it was, they threw stones into it. They then climbed down a narrow shaft and found themselves in a cave with walls covered in paintings of animals that seemed ready to bolt from their hiding spots.

PAINTINGS 16 FEET HIGH

The cave walls are covered in paintings of extinct species of bison, oxen, bulls, horses, and deer, as well as people (likely hunters or shamans), traps, arrows, and abstract motifs. The largest paintings are nearly 17 feet high. This art belongs to the Périgord style from 30,000–13,000 BCE and has a characteristic twisted perspective. The animals are shown in profile, but their horns are depicted from the front.

ANIMAL GODS

This cave, known as the "Sistine Chapel of Prehistory," was likely a shrine rather than a living space. The paintings may have served as a way to ensure success in hunting, or they could represent animal deities positioned as a map of the prehistoric night sky—an early zodiac of sorts. No one knows for sure.

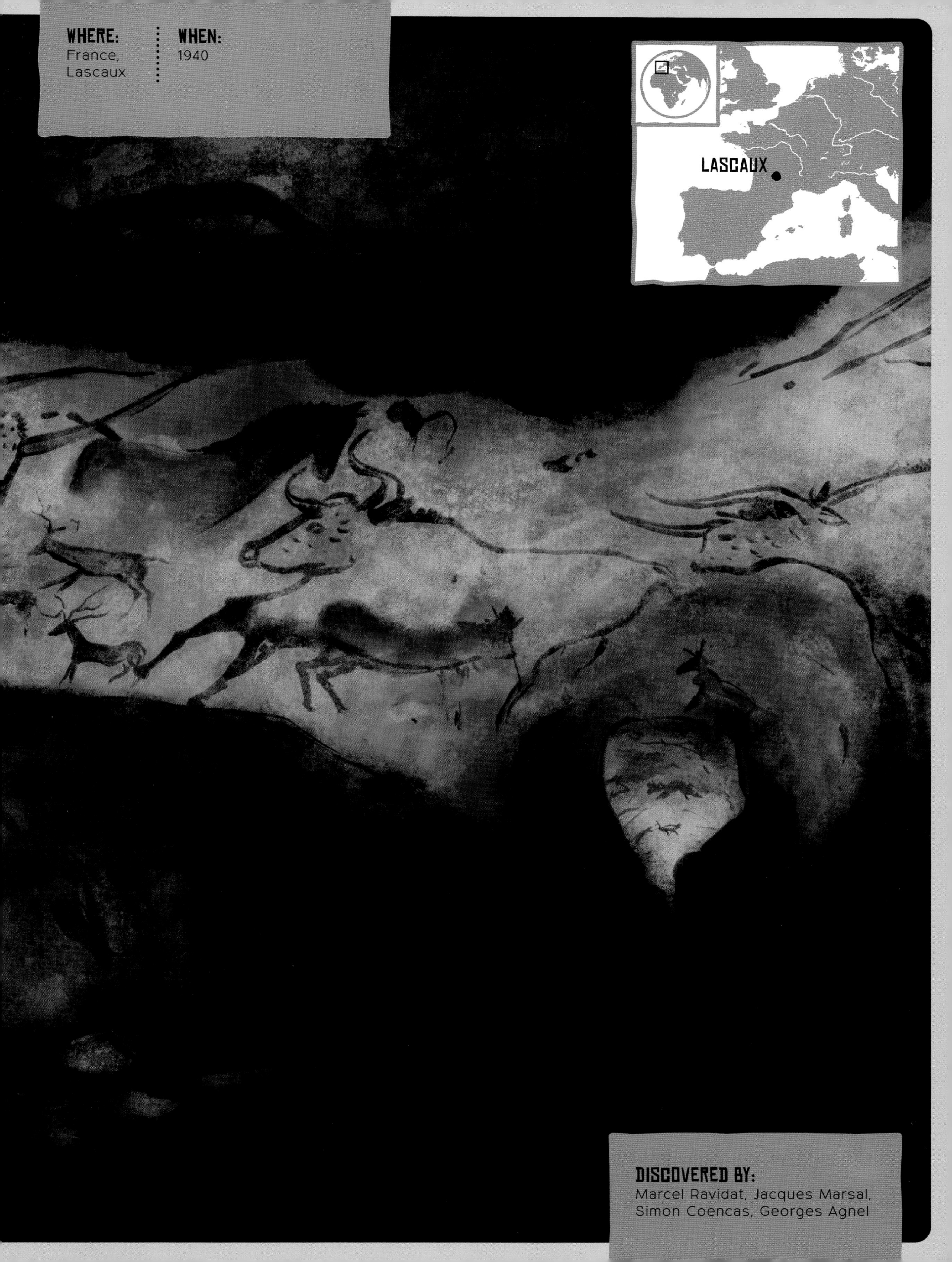
WHERE:
France, Lascaux
WHEN:
1940
LASCAUX
DISCOVERED BY:
Marcel Ravidat, Jacques Marsal, Simon Coencas, Georges Agnel

DEAD SEA SCROLLS

OLDEST COPIES OF TEXTS FROM THE OLD TESTAMENT

AN UNEXPECTED DISCOVERY

In the late 1940s, some young Bedouin goatherds were taking care of their animals near Qumran, the site of an old settlement, when they found an interesting-looking opening in a cliff. They dropped a stone into the hole and found out it was deep, and they wanted to know if it led anywhere. Imagine their surprise when they ended up in a cave with big earthenware vessels on the cave floor! Seven of these pots contained 2,000-year-old scrolls made of parchment and papyrus.

DISCOVERED BY:
Bedouin goatherds

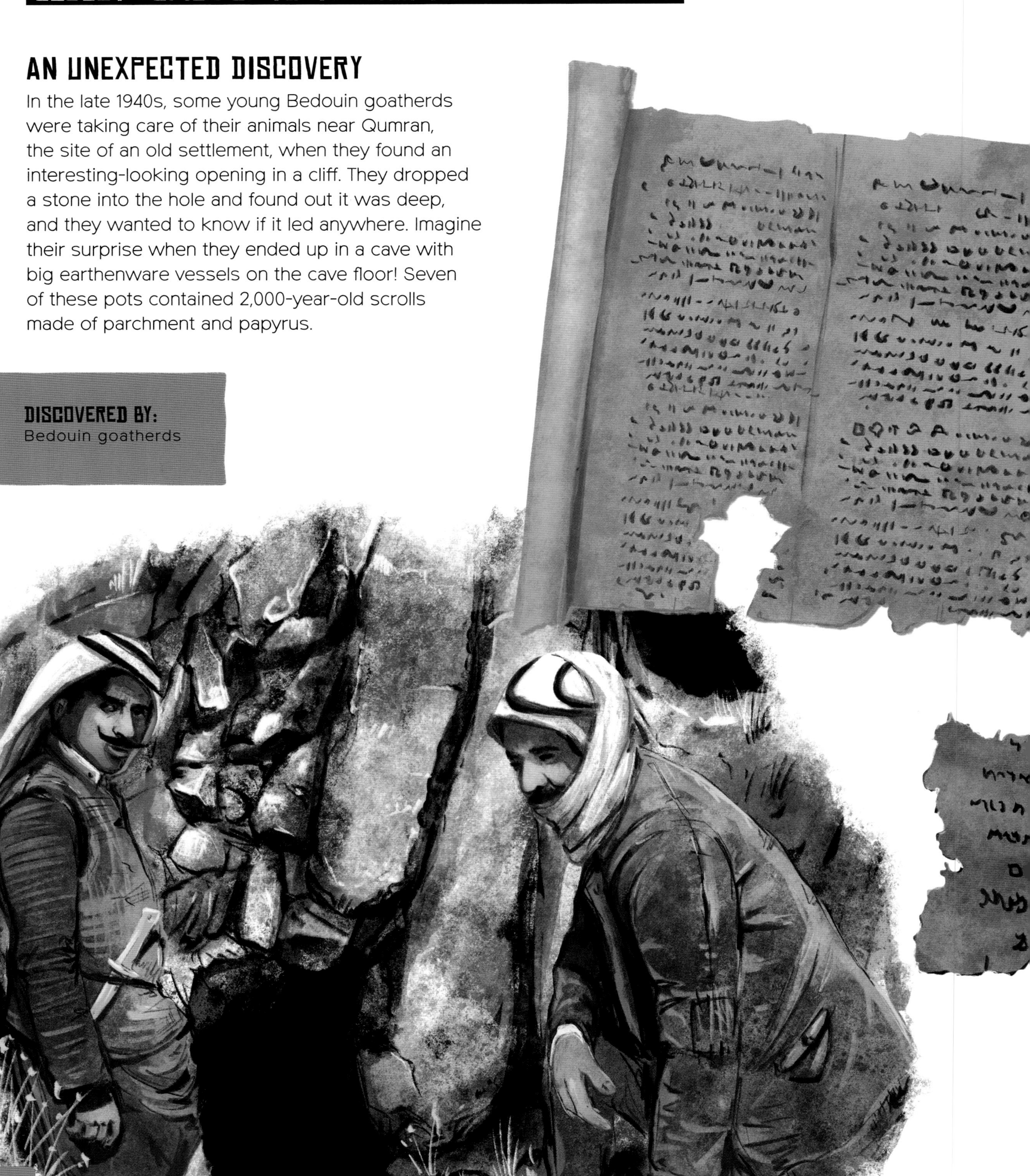

THE ISAIAH SCROLL CONTAINS ALMOST THE ENTIRE BOOK OF ISAIAH, WHICH TELLS OF THE FATE OF THE CITY OF JERUSALEM.

A COPPER SCROLL

Most of the texts are written on parchment or papyrus. The unique Copper Scroll is a list of places where gold and silver were buried or hidden. Fragments and scroll texts in ancient Hebrew and Aramaic are still being discovered in Qumran, and the Scrolls are still the subject of scholarly research.

WHERE: Qumran, Judean Desert

WHEN: 1947

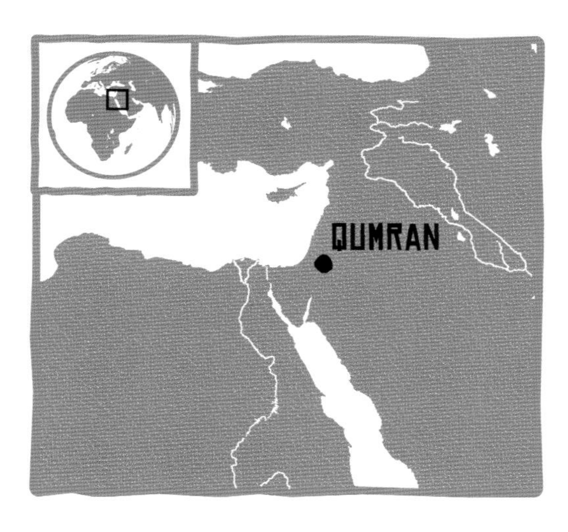

CONTENTS OF THE SCROLLS

It's believed that the manuscripts were made by a community of Jewish people who lived in Qumran between 150 BCE and 70 CE, when Roman soldiers destroyed their settlement. The scrolls are a record of sacred texts from the Old Testament and also writings for establishing rules and regulations for the community, including religious writings not in the Bible.

BUST OF NEFERTITI

Nefertiti (nέfərtíjtɪj)

WHERE: Egypt, Amarna

WHEN: 1912

AN IMPORTANT WORK OF ART DATING FROM THE REIGN OF THE PHARAOH AKHENATEN. REPRESENTATIVE OF THE AMARNA STYLE.

WHAT COULD IT BE?

First to appear in the sand was a bare neck the color of human skin, with red ribbons painted around it. The neck was followed by part of the chest and a wig fit for a queen. After that, the long process of uncovering and freeing the rest of the bust began. When the head of the famous Nefertiti was revealed in all its glory, archeologists led by Ludwig Borchardt were overcome with excitement. One of the most beautiful works of Ancient Egyptian art had seen the light of day once more.

THE BUST'S ORIGINS

The 20-inch-high limestone bust of the lovely wife of Pharaoh Akhenaten is most likely the work of court sculptor Thutmose. Experts believe that the bust in question was a model from which Thutmose created other likenesses of the queen—a woman who ruled Egypt with her husband in the 14th century BCE.

NEW ART

The reign of Pharaoh Akhenaten is often mentioned in history books for a groundbreaking religious reform that resulted in the worship of only one god—Aten, the sun god. Works of art produced during this period of religious change were characteristically realistic, even naturalistic, and depicted the everyday lives of Egyptians, while earlier religious themes receded into the background.

DISCOVERED BY:
German archeologist
Ludwig Borchardt

TUTANKHAMUN'S STEPMOTHER

Nefertiti means "the beautiful woman has come." She was a famous and powerful queen of Ancient Egypt, and also the stepmother of Tutankhamun. The limestone bust of her, wearing a high blue crown, can be seen at the Neues Museum in Berlin.

BUST

MORTAL REMAINS OF QUEEN NEFERTITI

DISCOVERED BY:
laborer Josef Seidl,
field engineer Emanuel Dania

WHERE:
Czech Republic,
Pálava hills

WHEN:
1925

VENUS OF DOLNÍ VĚSTONICE

VENUS OF DOLNÍ VĚSTONICE

Dolní Věstonice (dɔl nyi ˈvyɛ stɔ nyɪ tsɛ)

THE WORLD'S OLDEST CLAY FIGURINE – CRUCIAL FOR DETERMINING THE BEGINNINGS OF CERAMICS.

A PRECIOUS THING REVEALED

While digging in the Pálava hills, a region known for its mammoth hunters, Josef Seidl and Emanuel Dania found a broken figurine that was 4.5 inches tall. They had no idea how valuable it was. It wasn't until Moravian archeologist Karel Absolon returned from abroad that the importance of the *Venus of Dolní Věstonice* was revealed.

STILL A MYSTERY

The *Venus of Dolní Věstonice* was almost literally resurrected from the ashes. It spent an incredible 25,000 to 30,000 years in a fireplace. The unknown sculptor made it from loess clay mixed with water and fired at a low temperature. Scholars still wonder what it was for. Its large breasts and wide hips suggest it was as a symbol of femininity. Many other Venuses have a pregnant belly, symbolizing fertility.

THE *VENUS OF WILLENDORF* IS SIMILARLY FAMOUS

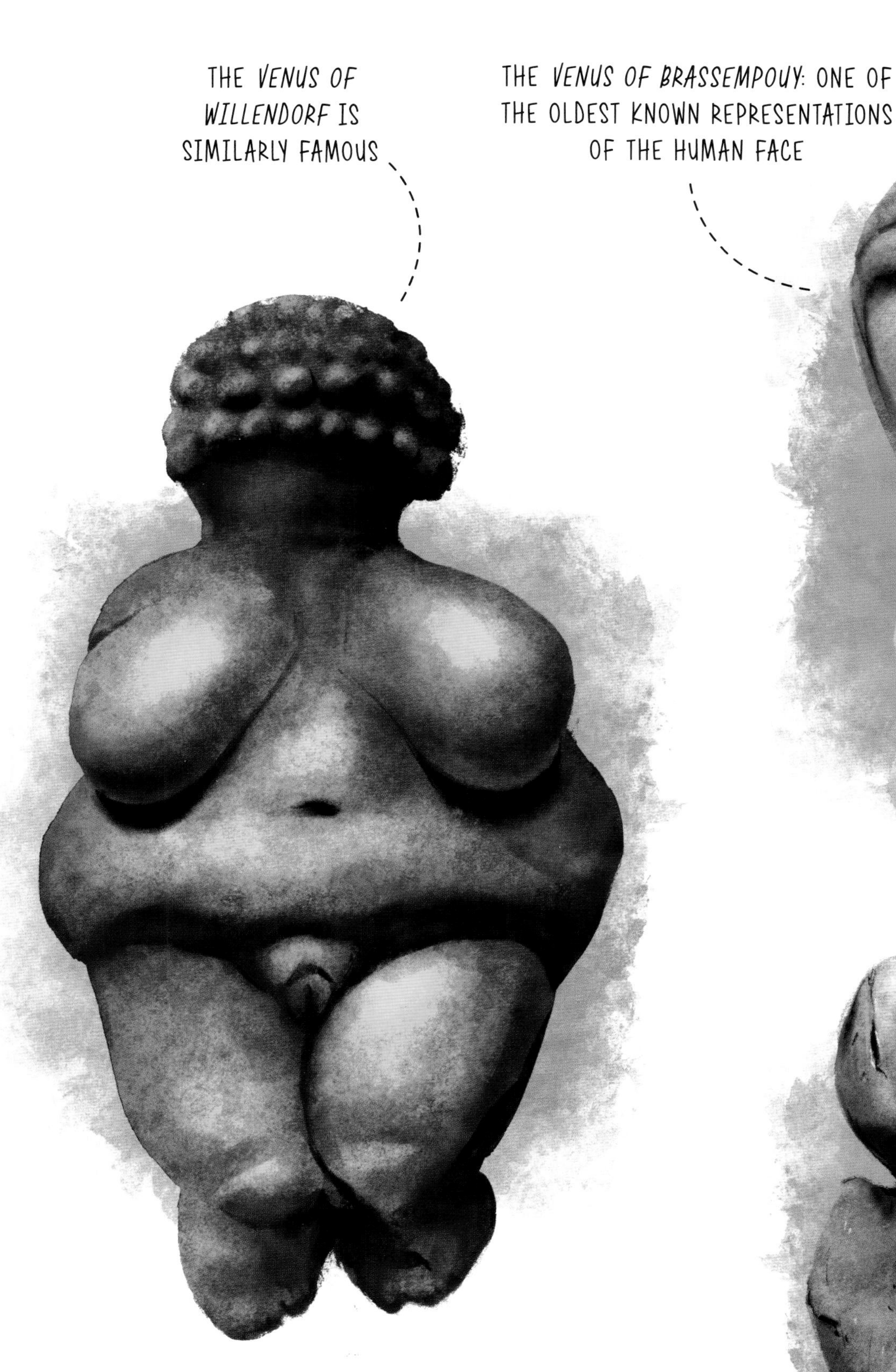

THE *VENUS OF BRASSEMPOUY*: ONE OF THE OLDEST KNOWN REPRESENTATIONS OF THE HUMAN FACE

VENUS OF HOHLE FELS

NOT THE ONLY VENUS

The *Venus of Dolní Věsto*nice is not the only prehistoric Venus. The oldest one—the *Venus of Hohle Fels*—is only 2 inches tall. It was carved from a woolly mammoth bone 40,000 years ago. The next oldest is the *Venus of Galgenberg,* which was made from green serpentine rock over 30,000 years ago.

DISCOVERED BY:
Josef Šlajchrt and
field watchman Štěpán Jeřábek

WHERE:
Czech Republic,
Mšecké Žehrovice

WHEN:
1943

MŠECKÉ ŽEHROVICE HEAD

Mšecké Žehrovice (mʃɛtskɛ ʒɛ hrɔ vyɪ tsɛ)

A UNIQUE CELTIC WORK OF ART UNLIKE ANYTHING ELSE IN THE WORLD.

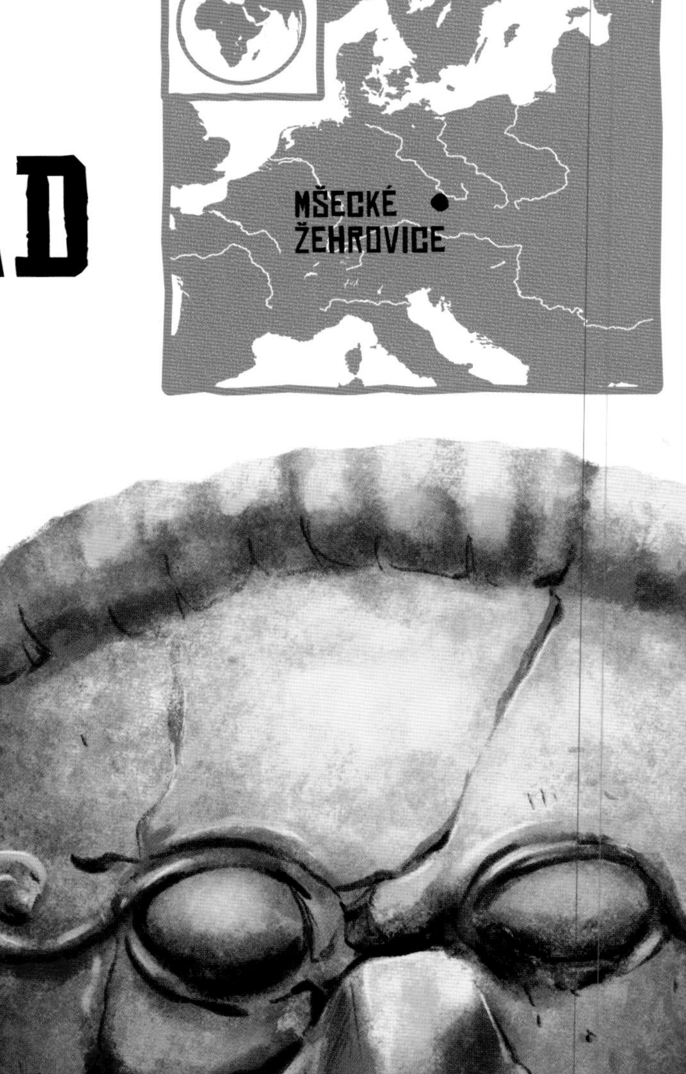

CATCH HIM!

On May 19, 1943, Josef Šlajchrt and his dad went to their sandpit, intent on catching a thief who had been stealing their sand. Although the thief got away before they could catch him, in the hole left by the thief, the Šlajchrts made an important discovery—fragments of a unique sculpture from the latter half of the 3rd century BCE, when the Celts lived in Bohemia. The final piece of the puzzle was provided by field watchman Štěpán Jeřábek, who checked out the discovery site one more time that same day.

THE HEAD WAS PROBABLY THAT OF A DRUID.

FAMOUS HEAD

Flat face, almond eyes, small nose, wavy eyebrows, striking twisted mustache—this is the face of the man of marl (a kind of earthy material). This realistic rendering even has a distinctive Celtic adornment, a neckband called a torques worn by upper-class men and women. The detail and realism make this Celtic head a unique work that is very different from the stone heads of the La Tène culture of ancient Gaul.

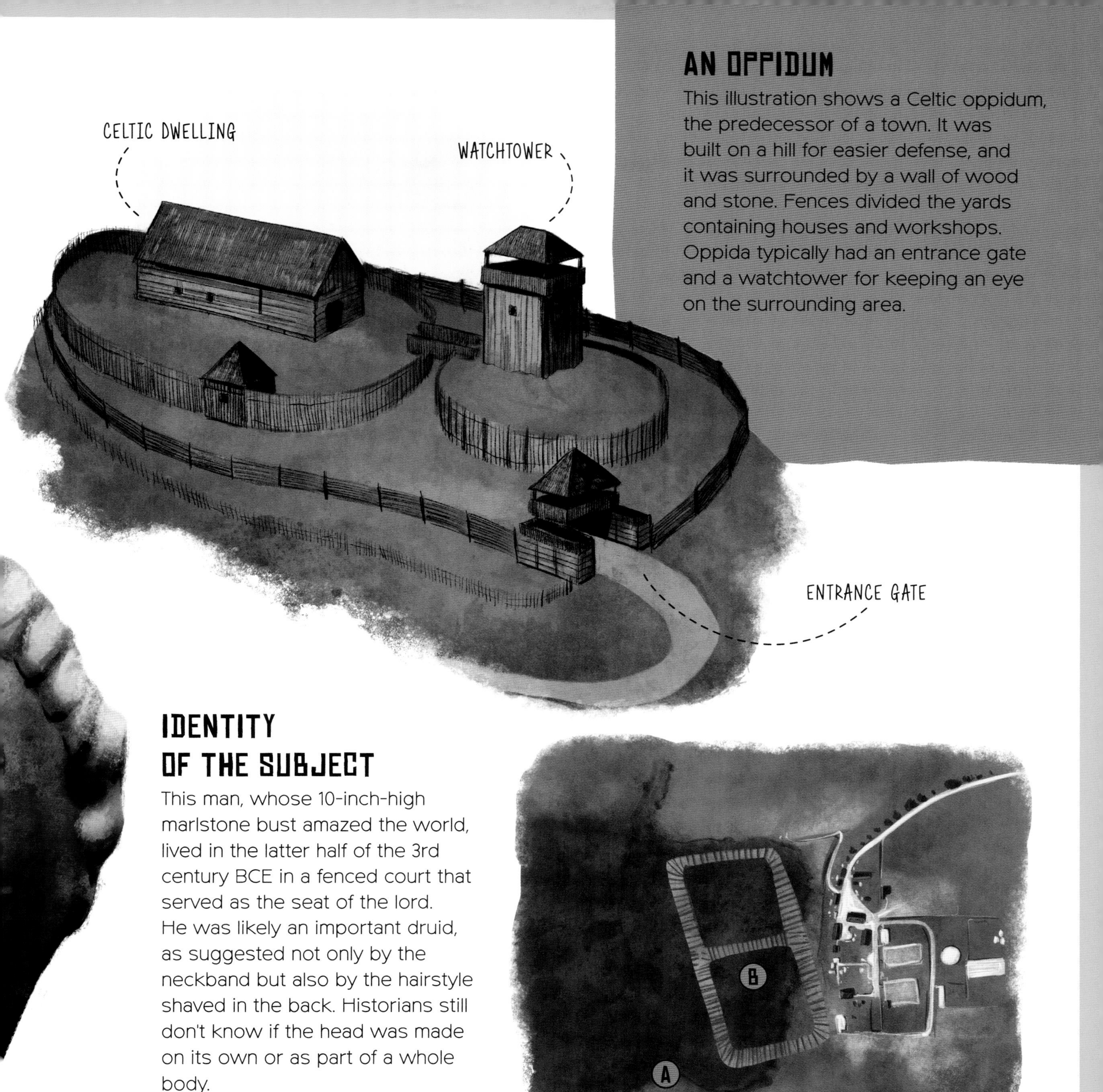

AN OPPIDUM

This illustration shows a Celtic oppidum, the predecessor of a town. It was built on a hill for easier defense, and it was surrounded by a wall of wood and stone. Fences divided the yards containing houses and workshops. Oppida typically had an entrance gate and a watchtower for keeping an eye on the surrounding area.

IDENTITY OF THE SUBJECT

This man, whose 10-inch-high marlstone bust amazed the world, lived in the latter half of the 3rd century BCE in a fenced court that served as the seat of the lord. He was likely an important druid, as suggested not only by the neckband but also by the hairstyle shaved in the back. Historians still don't know if the head was made on its own or as part of a whole body.

WHO WERE THE DRUIDS?

Druids were important figures for the Celts. They performed the functions of priests, poets, seers, shamans, and judges. The word *druid* can be translated as "knower of oak."

WHAT WAS THE HEAD FOR?

This map of the discovery site of the Mšecké Žehrovice Head Ⓐ shows the remains of a Celtic cult building Ⓑ. The religious nature of this building supports the theory that the head is that of a druid. Cult sites were used for observing religious rituals and ceremonies.

VENUS DE MILO

(vi nəs də ˈmaɪ loʊ)

AN ANTIQUE SCULPTURE OF GREAT BEAUTY.

THERE'S A WOMAN LYING HERE!

"There's a woman lying here in pieces!" On April 8, 1820, a poor peasant on the island of Milos may have said these very words to himself. Then he pulled two pieces from the ancient ruins on the edge of his land. They turned out to be part of a marble statue that was over 6 feet tall. Nearby, the peasant found one of her hands, which was holding an apple. "I'll finally be rich!" he surely muttered. Later that month, he sold the precious discovery to the Marquis de Riffarde, the French consul—for much less than it was worth, it should be added.

IN FRANCE

With great ceremony, the Marquis conveyed the beautiful statue to the court of the French king. That's how the magnificent torso of the goddess Aphrodite (sculpted between 120 and 100 BCE) ended up in the Louvre, where it is admired to this day.

WHERE:
Greek,
island of Milos

WHEN:
1820

SENSUAL BEAUTY

It's clear from a glance at the *Venus de Milo* that Ancient Greek sculptors sought to capture and express feminine charm. The body is full and youthful. The beautiful, unsmiling face has an expression of seriousness—perhaps because the apple she was holding in her missing hand symbolized the age-old Parisian question: What is most important in life? Should I choose power and success or love?

ORIGINAL APPEARANCE OF THE STATUE

The subject's weight is on the right leg, which is hidden in the folds of the robe. The left knee is slightly bent. The right hand evidently held the robe. The left arm was raised, and its hand held an apple. Since the statue's right side is rendered in greater detail than the left, the artist probably intended it to be viewed in profile.

DISCOVERED BY:
a poor peasant

PIRI REIS MAP

Piri Reis (pɪrɪ riz)

ACCURATE MAPPING OF ANTARCTICA 300 YEARS BEFORE ITS DISCOVERY.

BEHOLD, AN OLD MAP!

In September 1929, German theologian Gustav Adolf Deissmann began organizing and cataloging the volumes and other items in the library of Topkapi Palace in Istanbul. He made sure to include unused and discarded materials, and it was among these that he found a file of old maps. One of these maps was drawn on gazelle skin parchment. When Deissmann saw that it was dated 1513 and drawn by Turkish cartographer Ahmet Muhiddin Piri, he couldn't believe his eyes.

ICELESS ANTARCTICA

Piri, also known as Piri Reis, was an admiral of the Turkish fleet, a seasoned sailor, and an experienced cartographer. He based his map on much older maps from the time of the Ptolemaic dynasty, from Portugal, from Arabia, and even one by Christopher Columbus. On his map, Piri Reis shows in detail the west coast of Africa, the east coast of South America, and—amazingly—the north coast of Antarctica, without its cover of ice.

MAKING THE IMPOSSIBLE POSSIBLE

It was Piri Reis's depiction of Antarctica without its cover of ice that really impressed Deissmann. That's because Antarctica wasn't discovered until 1820, long after Piri Reis's death! What's more, this ice-free Antarctica was shown as it was almost 6,000 years ago. The map that Piri Reis used couldn't have been younger than that. But which highly advanced ancient civilization could have reached Antarctica in the early years of civilization in Mesopotamia?

DISCOVERED BY:
German theologian Gustav Adolf Deissmann

WHERE:
Turkey, Istanbul

WHEN:
1929

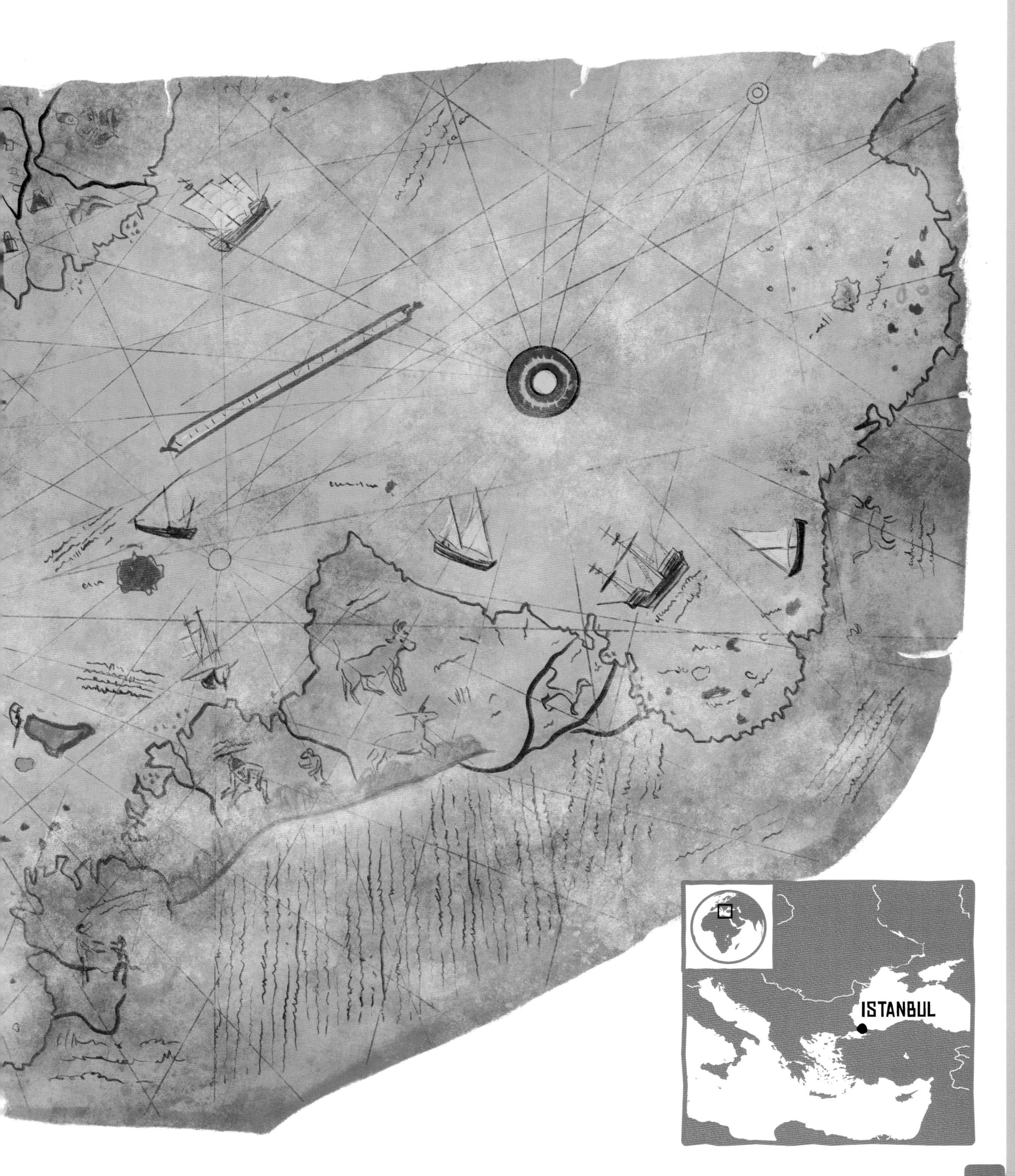

ANCIENT EGYPTIAN BARIS SHIP

Baris (bæɹɪs)

WHERE: Egypt, Nile River

WHEN: 2019

EGYPT

PROOF OF THE EXISTENCE OF AN ANCIENT EGYPTIAN SHIP DESCRIBED BY THE GREEK PHILOSOPHER HERODOTUS.

SHIPS ON THE NILE

Two and a half thousand years ago, special river ships made of acantha wood, with a hull in the shape of a half-crescent and sails made of papyrus, were common along the Nile River. Sailors used them to transport wood, fish, and stone. These ships were up to 92 feet long, so they were also suitable for transporting soldiers and their weapons. The Greek philosopher Herodotus was so impressed by these ships that he mentioned them in his famous work, *Herodoti Historiae*.

CAN WE BELIEVE HERODOTUS?

Herodotus may have written about long Egyptian river ships of the "baris" type, but how could scientists believe his report if not a single piece of such a ship had ever been found?

GOT IT!

In autumn 2019, the mystery of these Egyptian vessels was finally solved when archeologists found what they had long sought: an Ancient Egyptian ship of unique design. It was made of thick, strong boards of acantha wood that were about 3 feet long, stacked together like bricks and attached by tough pins to ribs that were over 6 feet long. It was steered by a rudder passed through two holes in the ship's stern.

RECONSTRUCTION OF THE SHIP

PERIOD DRAWINGS OF A BARIS SHIP

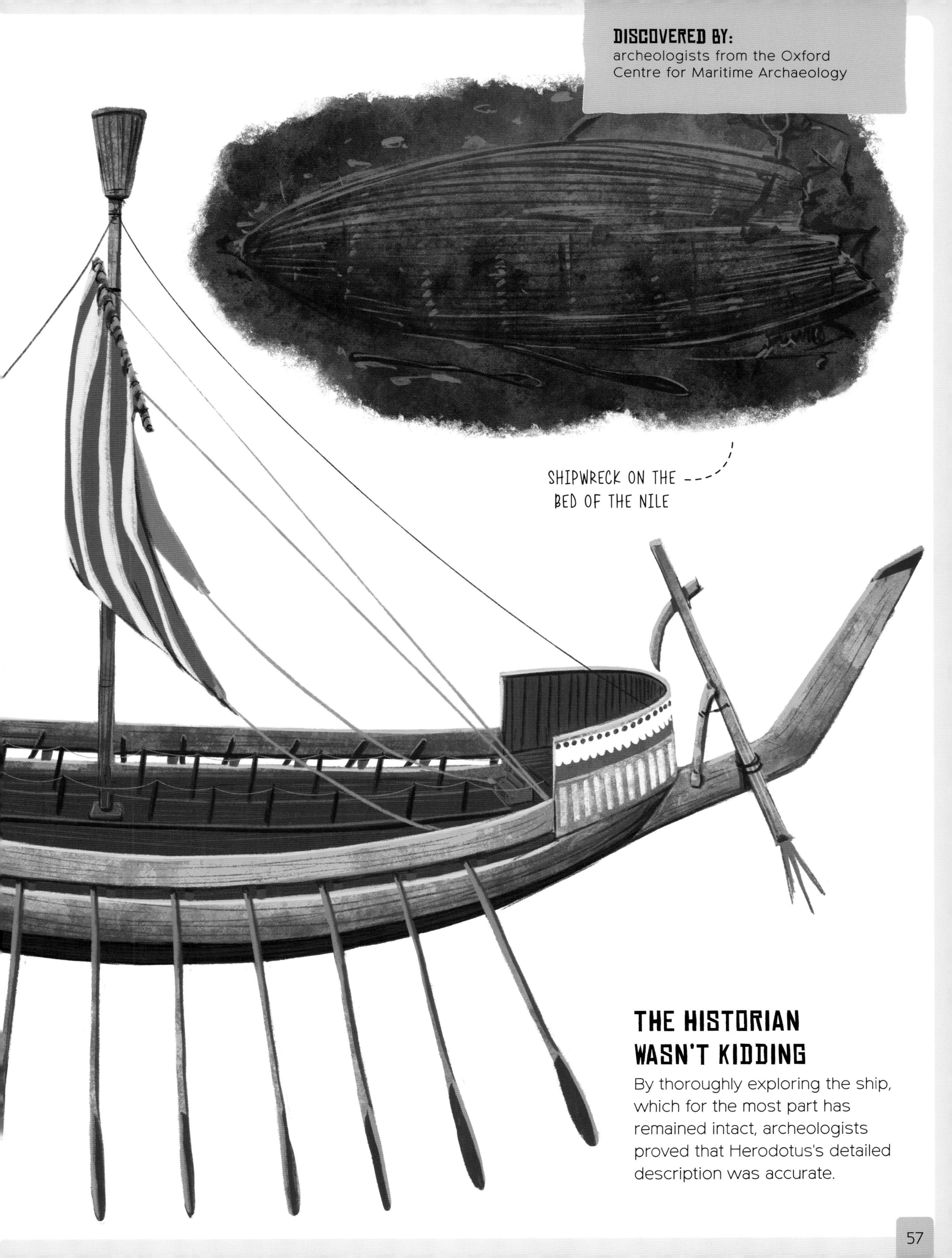

DISCOVERED BY:
archeologists from the Oxford Centre for Maritime Archaeology

THE HISTORIAN WASN'T KIDDING

By thoroughly exploring the ship, which for the most part has remained intact, archeologists proved that Herodotus's detailed description was accurate.

WHYDAH GALLY PIRATE SHIP

Whydah Gally (wájdə 'gæli)

ONE OF THE FIRST SHIPS IN AMERICAN WATERS WE KNOW FOR SURE TO HAVE BEEN IN PIRATE HANDS.

GOT IT!

Barry Clifford had to go only 14 feet below the surface of the Atlantic Ocean to perform his painstaking examination of a ship lying in layer after layer of sand. But what an adventure this examination must have been! After all, you don't find a real pirate ship every day. Thanks to Barry Clifford, the *Whydah Gally* has revealed its secrets to us.

A SHIP PACKED WITH GOLD

The *Whydah Gally* was built in 1715 as a slave ship, commissioned by British merchant Humphry Morice. It transported gold and other valuables to Africa, where it exchanged its load for ivory and—since the unspeakably brutal slave trade would not be outlawed in Britain until 1807—enslaved people. Next, the ship sailed on to the Caribbean, where it took on precious metals and valuable commodities like sugar, rum, rare spices, and medicine.

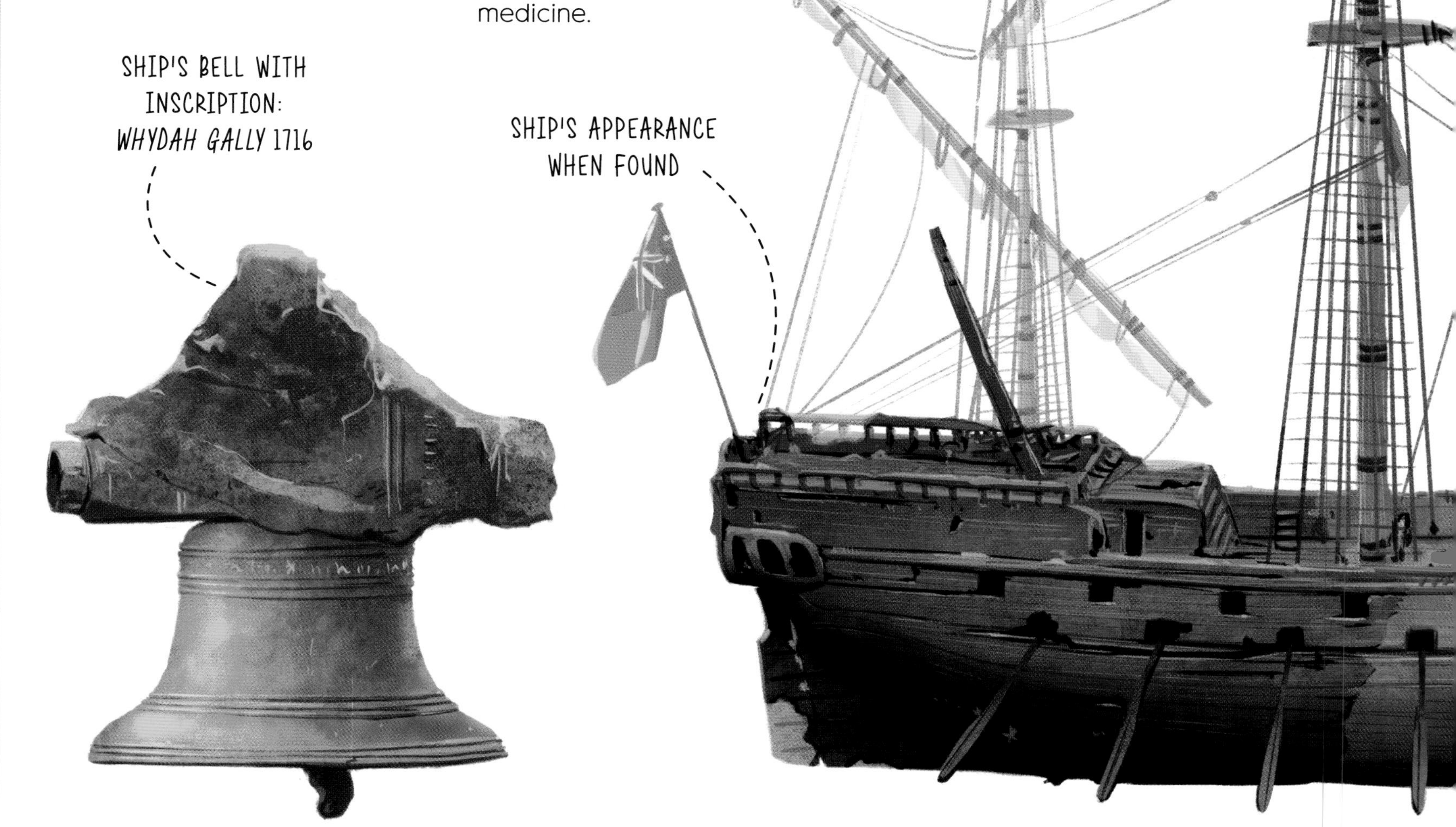

IN THE PIRATES' VIEWFINDER

It's hardly surprising that pirates targeted the *Whydah Gally*, a major merchant ship packed with valuables and enslaved people. After all, the 18th century was the golden age of piracy. So it came to pass that in 1717, the *Whydah Gally* was captured by the pirate Samuel Bellamy. Soon, there were even more riches on board, in the form of pirate loot. It's said that the pirates of the *Whydah Gally* seized weapons, plus gold and silver weighing 20,000 pounds, from 50 ships.

WHERE: USA, Atlantic Ocean, Cape Cod

WHEN: 1984

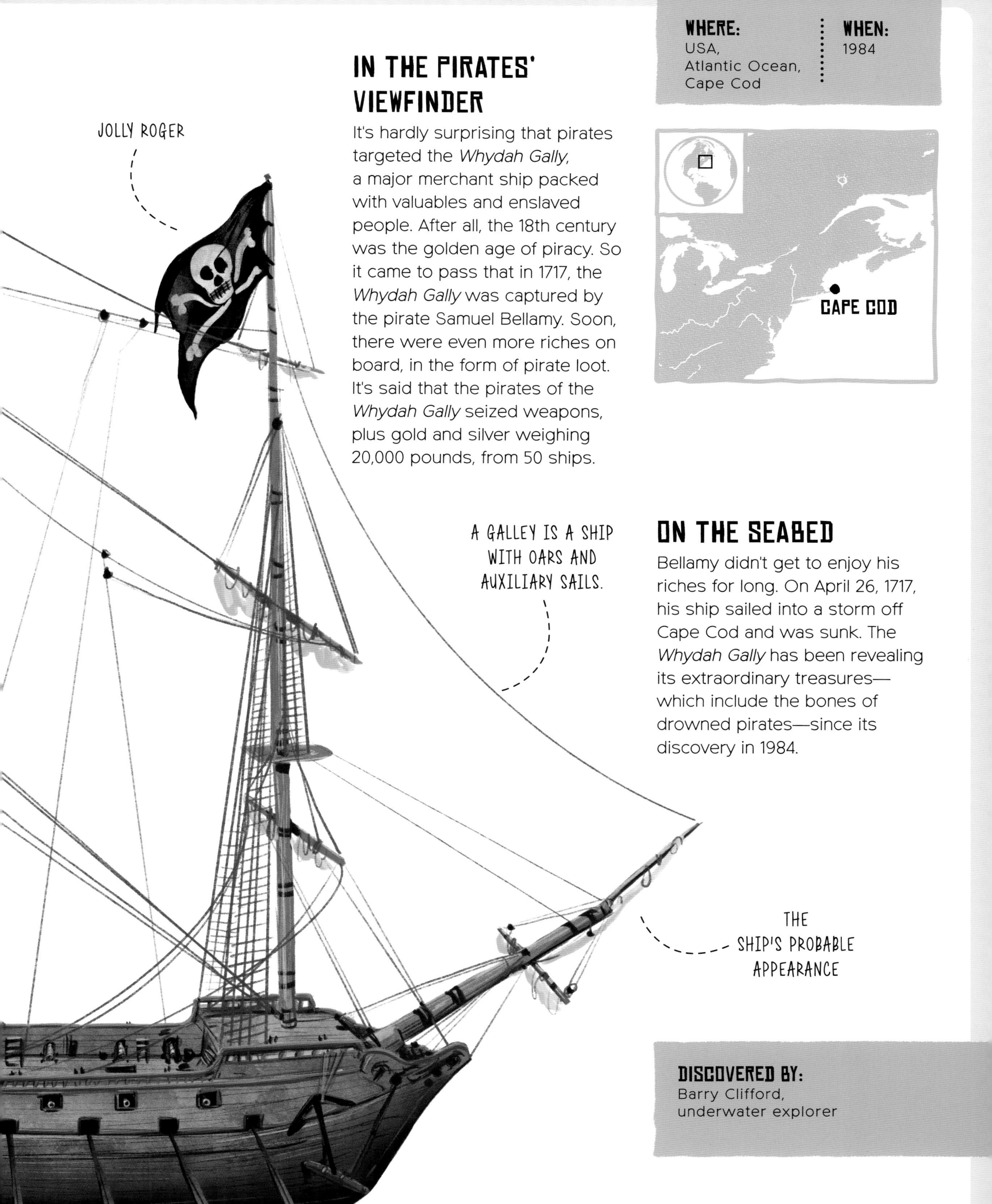

ON THE SEABED

Bellamy didn't get to enjoy his riches for long. On April 26, 1717, his ship sailed into a storm off Cape Cod and was sunk. The *Whydah Gally* has been revealing its extraordinary treasures—which include the bones of drowned pirates—since its discovery in 1984.

DISCOVERED BY:
Barry Clifford, underwater explorer

BLACK SEA SHIP

THE ONLY INTACT SHIPWRECK FROM ANTIQUITY EVER FOUND.

UNBELIEVABLE!

In 2018, when an international team of scientists from the Black Sea Maritime Archaeological Project reached the seabed, they couldn't believe what they were seeing: an Ancient Greek ship. It was over 2,400 years old and was in near perfect condition, with its mast, rudders, rowers' benches, and oars still in place. Who would have guessed that the ocean deep was hiding such an ancient treasure?

A MERCHANT SHIP

Experts think the ship is a type of merchant vessel that the Ancient Greeks often used—although we can only compare it with pictures of similar ships depicted on amphorae (ancient two-handled jars used to transport wine and olive oil) and other old pots. Its uniqueness makes the discovery all the more valuable. To protect it from damage, the ship stays on the seabed, where archeologists can explore it using remote-controlled submarines Ⓐ.

DISCOVERED BY:
an international team of scientists from the Black Sea Maritime Archaeological Project

WHERE:
Black Sea

WHEN:
2018

A MIRACLE WITHOUT OXYGEN

The 2,400-year-old, 5-foot-long Ancient Greek ship Ⓑ has remained just as it was when it sank, due to the lack of oxygen at a depth of over one mile.

THE SAN JOSÉ

(sæn həʊˈzeɪ)

FLAGSHIP OF THE SPANISH FLEET, CONTAINING MANY VALUABLE HISTORICAL ARTIFACTS.

WHERE: Colombia, Cartagena

WHEN: 2015

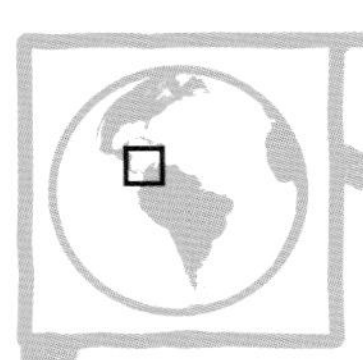

CARTAGENA

an international team
of scientists led by Roger Dooley

THE END OF A FAMOUS SHIP

The *San José* was a three-mast flagship of King Philip V of Spain's fleet. From 1701 to 1714, Philip V fought a long war against England over Spanish succession. During this conflict, in 1708, the enemy sank the galleon.

GUNS ON THE SEABED

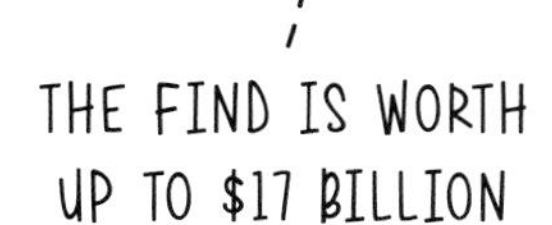

LET'S LEAVE IT DOWN THERE

In 2015, after a long and intensive search, an international research team finally discovered the "Holy Grail" of sunken shipwrecks. They found it buried under sediment, uncovering not only the gold but also works in bronze decorated with engravings of dolphins. This extremely valuable treasure remains at the bottom of the sea. Its location has not been made public.

SEA OF GOLD

Only 11 crewmembers were saved, while the rest of the 589 crewmembers, along with an enormous fortune of 11 million gold coins being transported from the Spanish colonies, went to a watery grave.

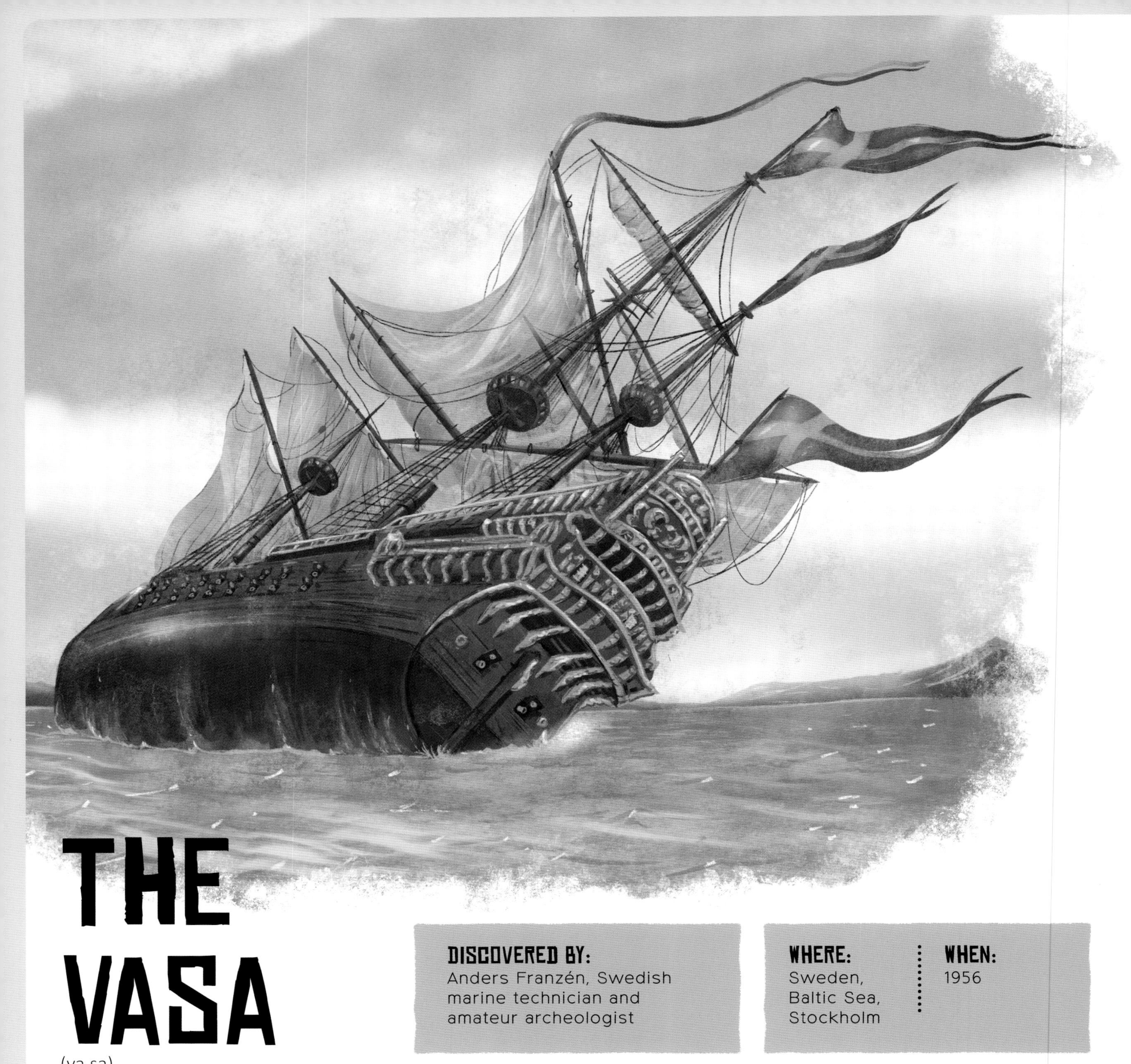

THE VASA

(va.sa)

DISCOVERED BY:
Anders Franzén, Swedish marine technician and amateur archeologist

WHERE:
Sweden, Baltic Sea, Stockholm

WHEN:
1956

SHIP SAID TO REPRESENT THE POWER OF THE SWEDISH KING.

SWEDEN'S PRIDE AND JOY

From 1625 to 1628, King Gustavus Adolphus of Sweden personally oversaw construction of the *Vasa*, a vessel that was said to be the largest and most heavily armed sailing ship of its time, and meant to demonstrate his power. During its construction, changes were made to the ship; the king demanded more cannons, despite the fact that the ship's design couldn't accommodate them.

THE MOST POWERFUL AND UNSINKABLE

The three-masted *Vasa* ended up with an impressive 64 cannons on board, along with all the necessary ammunition. However, before it was launched, the engineers chose not to conduct a stability test, since they were sure it would fail and they didn't want to risk the wrath of King Gustavus Adolphus.

SAILING OUT

On August 10, 1628, the *Vasa* set sail to great fanfare, with a ceremonial salvo from all 64 of its cannons marking the start of its maiden voyage. However, shortly after, the wind picked up and it began to sink. Within a short time, it was at the bottom of the sea, along with 30 officers and 150 crewmembers. The *Vasa*, the pride of Sweden, was supposed to go to battle against Poland, but it spent only a single day on the waves.

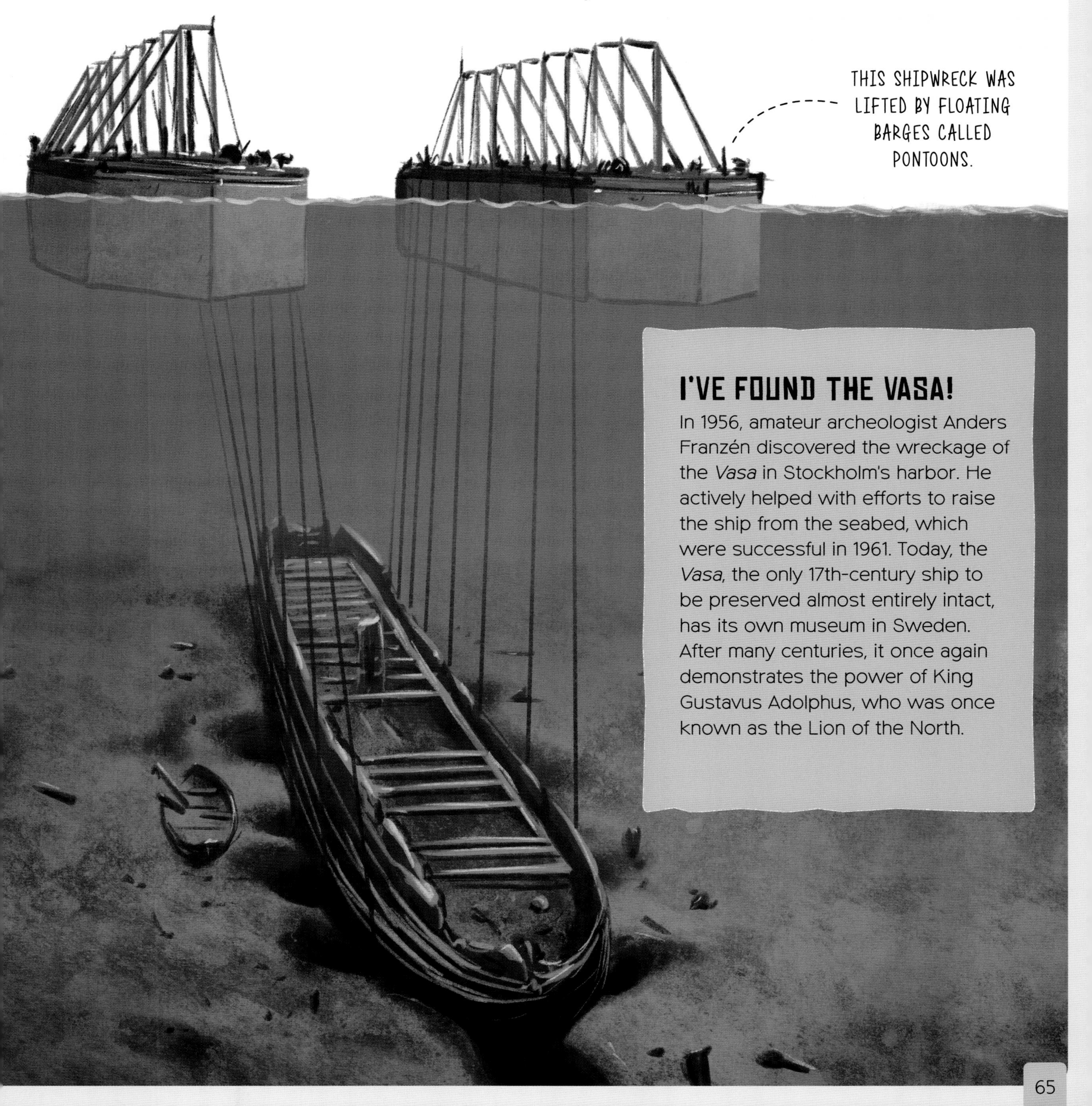

I'VE FOUND THE VASA!

In 1956, amateur archeologist Anders Franzén discovered the wreckage of the *Vasa* in Stockholm's harbor. He actively helped with efforts to raise the ship from the seabed, which were successful in 1961. Today, the *Vasa*, the only 17th-century ship to be preserved almost entirely intact, has its own museum in Sweden. After many centuries, it once again demonstrates the power of King Gustavus Adolphus, who was once known as the Lion of the North.

LIGHTHOUSE OF ALEXANDRIA

DISCOVERED BY:
French archeologist Jean-Yves Empereur

WHERE:
Egypt, Alexandria

WHEN:
1994

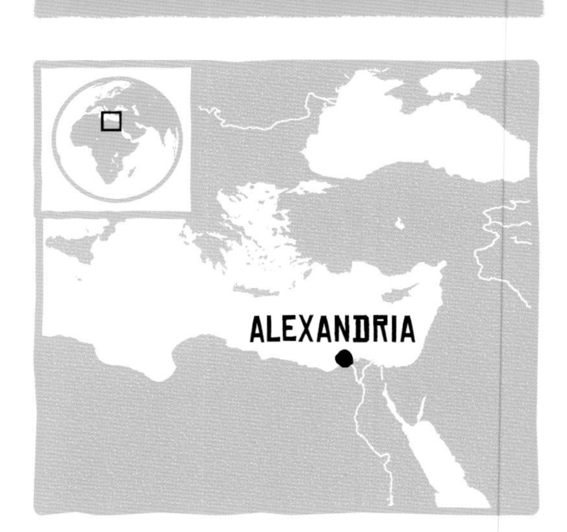

PROOF OF THE EXISTENCE OF ONE OF THE SEVEN WONDERS OF THE ANCIENT WORLD.

IS THIS TRULY A WONDER OF THE WORLD?

In the 1990s, plans were made to build a breakwater near the island of Pharos. Before work began, French archeologist Jean-Yves Empereur went to the site and discovered hundreds of large blocks of granite and plinths for statues, as well as fragments of columns, on the seabed. This led him to believe he had found the remains of the famous Lighthouse of Alexandria. The plans for the breakwater were thus abandoned.

IT REALLY WAS THERE!

Three thousand giant blocks of granite, plinths for statues, fragments of columns, and a 40-foot-high door for a monumental building were discovered. This building was believed to be 400 feet tall. In ancient times, its light was used to guide seafarers to the mainland from distances of up to 35 miles!

THE LIGHTHOUSE DEPICTED ON ALEXANDRIAN COINS FROM THE 2ND CENTURY BCE

RECORD-HOLDER OF THE ANCIENT WORLD

Ptolemy I Soter, the ruler of Egypt and founder of the Ptolemaic Dynasty, commissioned the construction of the lighthouse near Alexandria (Egypt's then-new capital) in the 4th century BCE. It was meant to be the tallest building in the ancient world.

DESTRUCTION OF THE LIGHTHOUSE

The Romans, ruled by Caesar Augustus (also known as Octavian), conquered Alexandria at the end of the 1st century BCE. The lighthouse suffered serious damage during the fighting and was further devastated by an earthquake in the 4th century. It received a final, fatal blow from an earthquake in 1326 and was gone forever as one of the Wonders of the Ancient World.

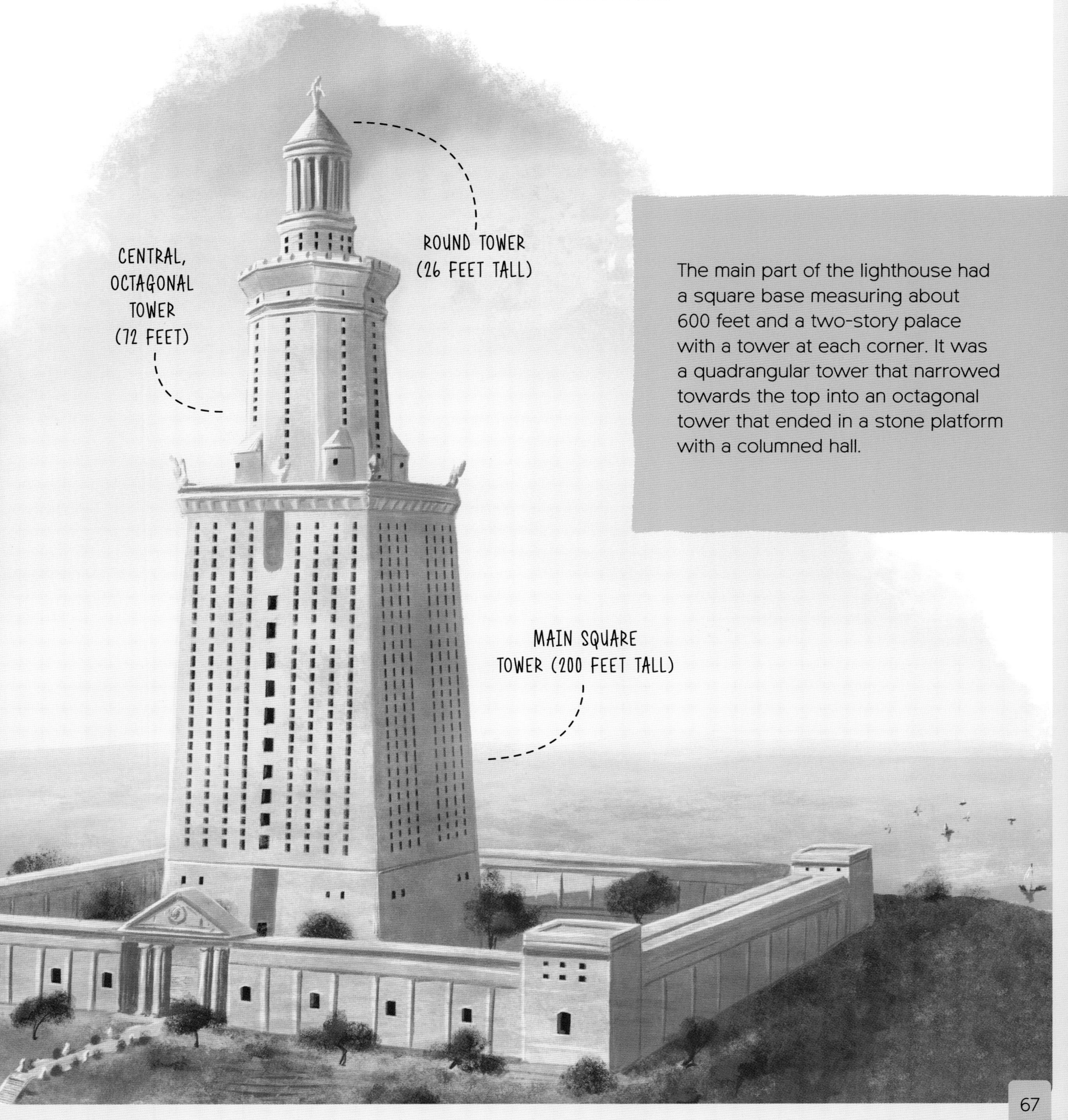

The main part of the lighthouse had a square base measuring about 600 feet and a two-story palace with a tower at each corner. It was a quadrangular tower that narrowed towards the top into an octagonal tower that ended in a stone platform with a columned hall.

THE YAMATO

(jɑːmətəʊ)

JAPANESE CRUISER DESTROYED IN WORLD WAR II – THE LARGEST SUNKEN BATTLESHIP EVER RECOVERED

WHERE: East China Sea

WHEN: 1982

A FLOATING FORTRESS

The Japanese battleship *Yamato* was meant to be—and was—the biggest battleship ever made. During World War II, it was the flagship of the Japanese emperor and had his seal. Even so, this magnificent floating fortress met a tragic end, sinking to the bottom of the sea along with 2,475 sailors. Only 269 of the large crew survived.

DISCOVERED BY:
a team of Japanese
and French scientists

FULL BATTLE DRESS

The *Yamato* was 850 feet long, 130 feet wide, and had a hull fitted with a 16-inch-thick steel armor plate. Its decks had three huge turrets, each with three main guns that could launch a projectile over a range of 25 miles, and 100 smaller guns. But in its five years as a battleship, it never saw action in naval conflict—the very reason it was built.

THE ULTIMATE SACRIFICE

The Japanese had kept the existence of the flagship of their Imperial Navy a strict secret and destroyed its plans after its demise. It was sacrificed at the end of World War II while defending the Japanese island of Okinawa, which it was tasked to protect until its destruction. Thus, the story of the battleship *Yamato* ended tragically on April 7, 1945. After sustaining around 20 direct hits in a two-hour attack by the U.S. Air Force, the *Yamato* sank to the seabed and met its end.

KUBLAI KHAN'S FLEET

Kublai Khan (kʉ́wblə káːn)

THE FLEET OF THE MONGOLIAN KHAN WAS DEFEATED BY JAPANESE SAMURAI AND NATURAL FORCES.

DISCOVERED BY:
Japanese archeologists from the University of the Ryukyus

WHERE: East China Sea

WHEN: 2011

THE WRATH OF KUBLAI KHAN

In 1259, Mongolia's mighty leader Kublai Khan conquered China and became its emperor. He then invaded and conquered Korea. Next on his list was Japan, which stood up to him. Kublai Khan was so angry at this resistance that he ordered the construction of a massive fleet of warships and sailed to Japan with them.

THE FIRST ATTACK

Kublai Khan and his fleet reached the coast of Japan in 1274. His planned conquest was met with unexpected resistance from Japanese samurai, who were aided by a powerful typhoon that dispersed a full third of Kublai Khan's fleet.

ARTIST'S IMPRESSION OF EVENTS

A SECOND ATTACK

On the second attempt, the great Mongolian conqueror arrived in Japan with 4,400 warships manned by 40,000 warriors. Although the Japanese were prepared for the attack, they expected the battle to be long and hard. So imagine their surprise when the entire mighty fleet vanished from view just as it was approaching their shores, as if by magic! Once again, they had a typhoon to thank.

QUICK WORK

Although Kublai Khan's ships seemed extremely threatening at first glance, closer inspection showed that many of them didn't have a deep keel, meaning they were unstable. They were built quickly but poorly, with predictably bad results.

INGLORIOUS REMAINS

All that's left of Kublai Khan's naval fleet are scraps—bulkheads, keels, timbers, firearms, pots, and the bones of drowned Mongolian warriors. These sad relics of Kublai Khan's expansionism are carefully examined by Japanese archeologists.

BATTLESHIP KARLSRUHE

Karlsruhe (kɑːlzruːə)

DISCOVERED BY:
Norwegian power grid operator Statnett

A UNIQUE WARSHIP FOUND PRACTICALLY INTACT.

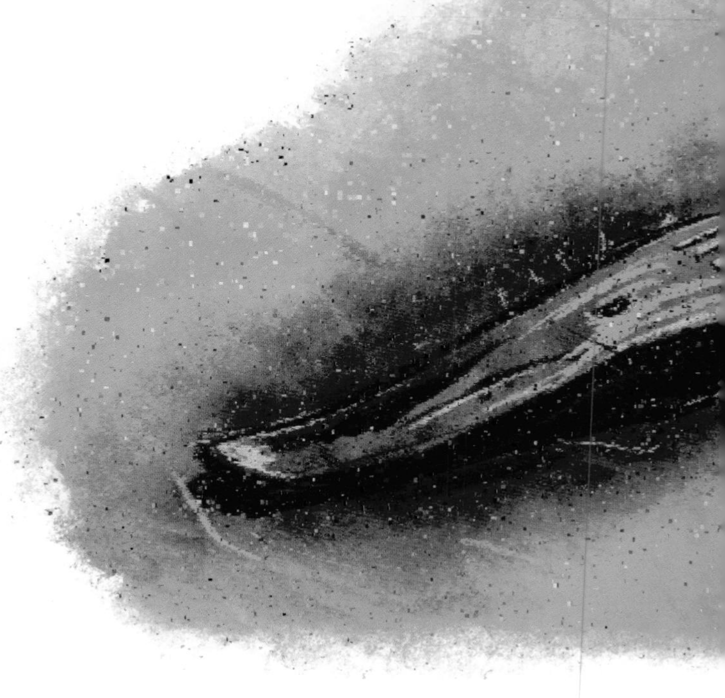

WHAT'S THAT DOWN THERE?

In 2017, employees of a Norwegian power grid company were laying underwater cables at the bottom of the North Sea when they stumbled upon the remains of an interesting ship. To chart and photograph the wreck, they sent down a special submarine. Close inspection revealed that the Statnett energy company had found the long-sought light cruiser *Karlsruhe*, one of Nazi Germany's flagships.

ATTACK ON NORWAY

The cruiser was 481 feet long and equipped with steam turbines and nine guns in three turrets. On April 9, 1940, it was on its way to Norway as part of Operation Weserübung, which aimed to invade Norway. Thick fog made it hard for the captain to steer the ship into the fjords. Then, before the Germans knew what was happening, the Norwegians fired on them from Odderoya Fortress. The British finished what the Norwegians started by hitting the cruiser with torpedoes, causing such serious damage that Karlsruhe's crew had to abandon ship. Later, the Germans sank it themselves.

LENGTH: 480 FEET

WHERE:
Norway,
North Sea

WHEN:
2017

BIOGRAPHY OF A CRUISER

Except for the damage caused by the torpedoes, the cruiser lying 1,607 feet underwater is practically intact. Built as the first of its type in 1926, it was launched a year later. One of the missions of its over 500-member crew before the start of World War II was patroling the Spanish coastline during the Spanish Civil War. Although *Karlsruhe* was built for combat, the invasion of Norway proved to be its end.

SCAN OF THE SHIPWRECK

DISCOVERED BY:
Norwegian students at the Marine Technology Centre

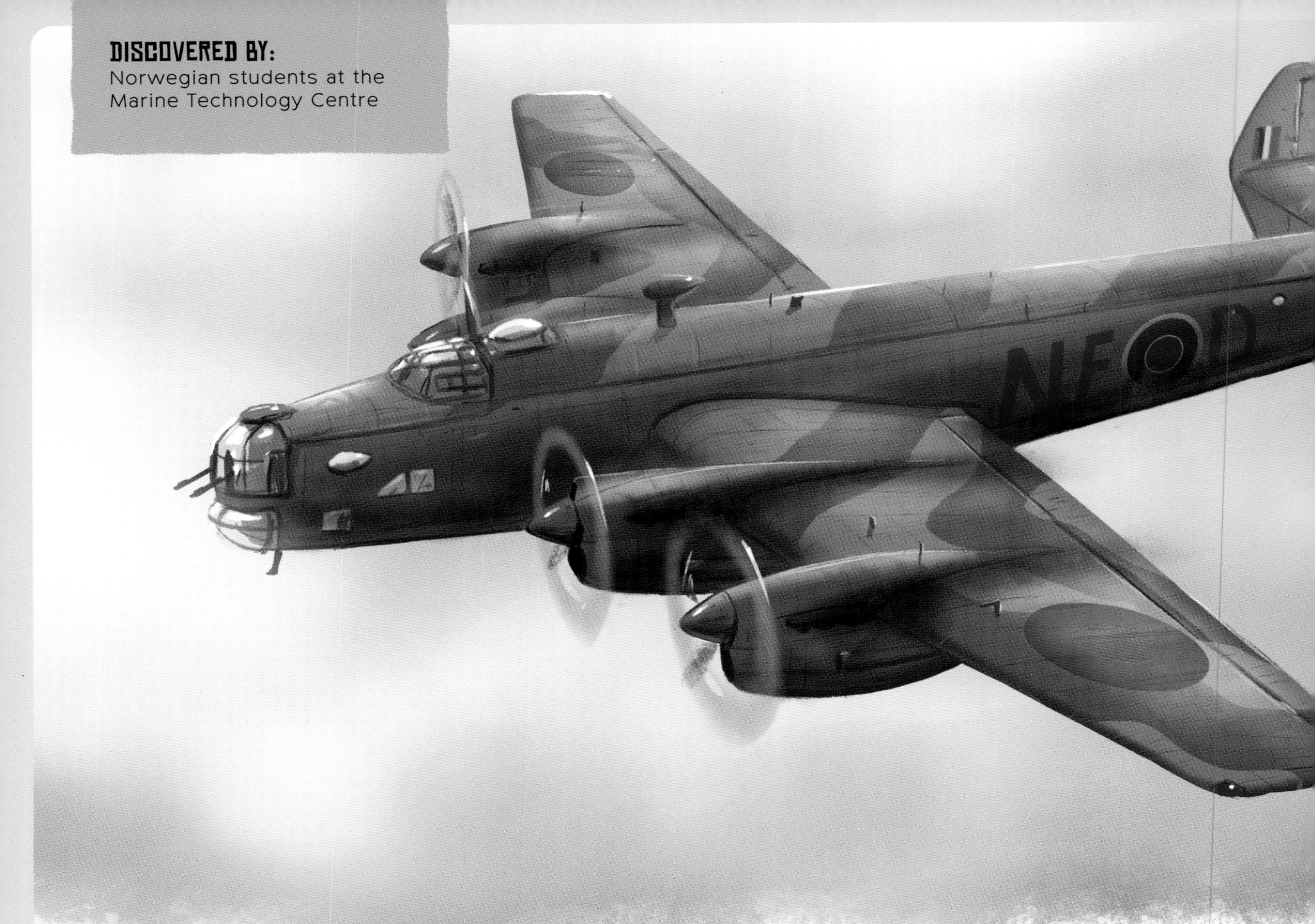

HALIFAX BOMBER

THE AIRCRAFT THAT ATTACKED THE GERMAN BATTLESHIP TIRPITZ.

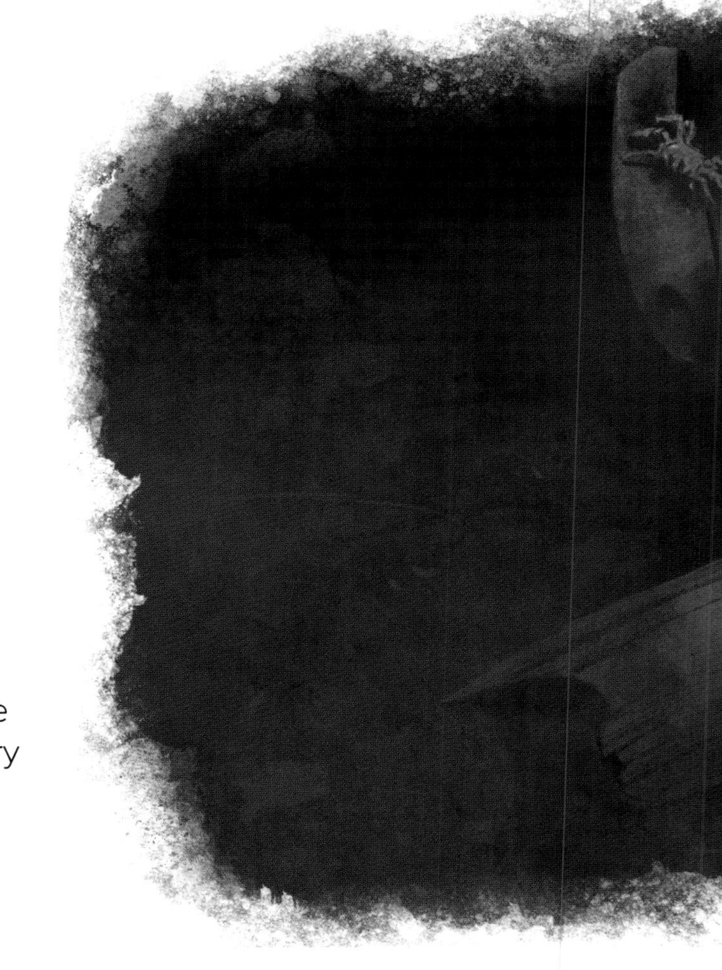

WHAT IS IT, SIR?

In 2014, six Norwegian students at the Marine Technology Centre entered the North Sea with no high hopes. It was just an ordinary practice exercise to test their knowledge of using underwater technologies. So imagine their amazement when they found the wreck of a World War II plane—a famous Halifax bomber!

WHERE: North Sea

WHEN: 2014

A DIGNIFIED WRECK

The students were truly shocked. The four-engine aircraft with its nose stuck in the sand had a wingspan of 98 feet. The fuselage was damaged by seawater, but otherwise the find was almost complete. Even the Merlin engine with wooden propellers was preserved.

THE GOAL: TO DESTROY THE GERMAN SHIPS TIRPITZ AND BISMARCK

Britain's Halifax bombers did their best to destroy the powerful German ship *Tirpitz*, which was hiding in the fjords of Norway. Several of the British planes were shot down in these attempts, ending up at the bottom of the sea. We believe that it ended its active life on April 26, 1942, on a mission to destroy the German battleship *Bismarck*. The crew of this Halifax—the pilot and the navigator—went to a watery grave with it.

THE TITANIC

WHERE: Atlantic Ocean
WHEN: 1985

THE WRECK OF THE LEGENDARY "UNSINKABLE" SHIP.

WILL I EVER FIND THE TITANIC?

Oceanographer Robert Ballard had been searching the ocean for almost two weeks when he finally succeeded: on September 1, 1985, he discovered the wreckage of the legendary "unsinkable" passenger liner *Titanic*. Screens below deck on the research vessel *Knorr* detected the first manmade objects—and then more and more, including a steam boiler. Commander Ballard had brought the *Titanic* back to us.

UNSUCCESSFUL SEARCHERS

Robert Ballard wasn't the only one drawn to searching for the final resting place of the unique passenger liner. In the 1960s, an English hosier named Douglas Woolley made several unsuccessful attempts. Texan oil magnate Jack Grimm did the same in the 1980s. The grand discovery was waiting for Ballard.

A FAMOUS BURIAL GROUND

The monumental hull lies in two pieces about 2,500 feet apart. The stern Ⓐ of the *Titanic* sank very quickly and sustained irreparable damage; the bow Ⓑ, however, is well preserved. Even so, this legendary ship will remain on the seabed until it completely disintegrates.

A KILLER ICEBERG

The "unsinkable" luxury oceangoing liner set out on its first and final voyage on April 10, 1912. Just four days later, it reportedly collided with an iceberg—a collision that would prove fatal. That same night, it and all the riches on board went to the bottom of the icy sea. As for the passengers and crew, 1,700 poor souls were buried with it, while 700 were lucky enough to survive.

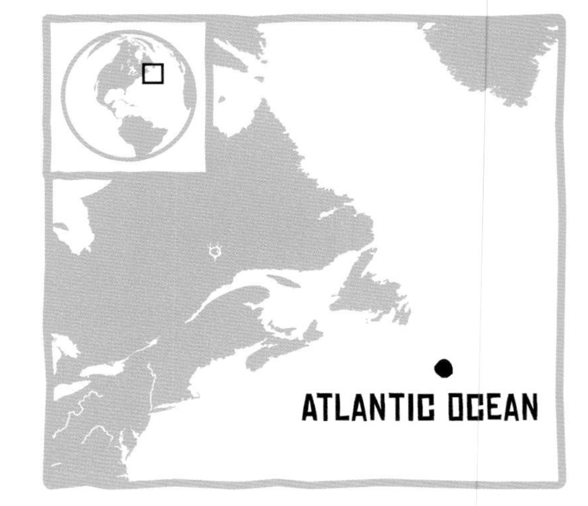

DISCOVERED BY:
oceanographer Robert Ballard

WHERE:
Egypt,
Valley of the Kings

WHEN:
1817

DISCOVERED BY:
Italian adventurer
Giovanni Battista Belzoni

TOMB OF PHARAOH SETI I

Pharaoh (fé:rəw) Seti (sɛtɪ)

THE VERY LARGEST ROYAL TOMB AT THE VALLEY OF THE KINGS.

AN EGYPTIAN ADVENTURE

Giovanni Battista Belzoni, a native of Padua, Italy, was always interested in invention and adventure. So he found himself in Egypt, where he joined the excavations led by Swiss researcher J. L. Burckhardt. On October 16, 1817, Belzoni discovered the entrance to the large, fully decorated tomb of Pharaoh Seti I.

LUXURY FIT FOR A PHARAOH

The burial chambers were approached through several porticoes. The pharaoh's body rested in the rear burial room, housed in a valuable alabaster sarcophagus beneath a unique vaulted ceiling covered in astronomical data that scientists are still attempting to decipher. Unfortunately, looters visited the tomb in earlier centuries.

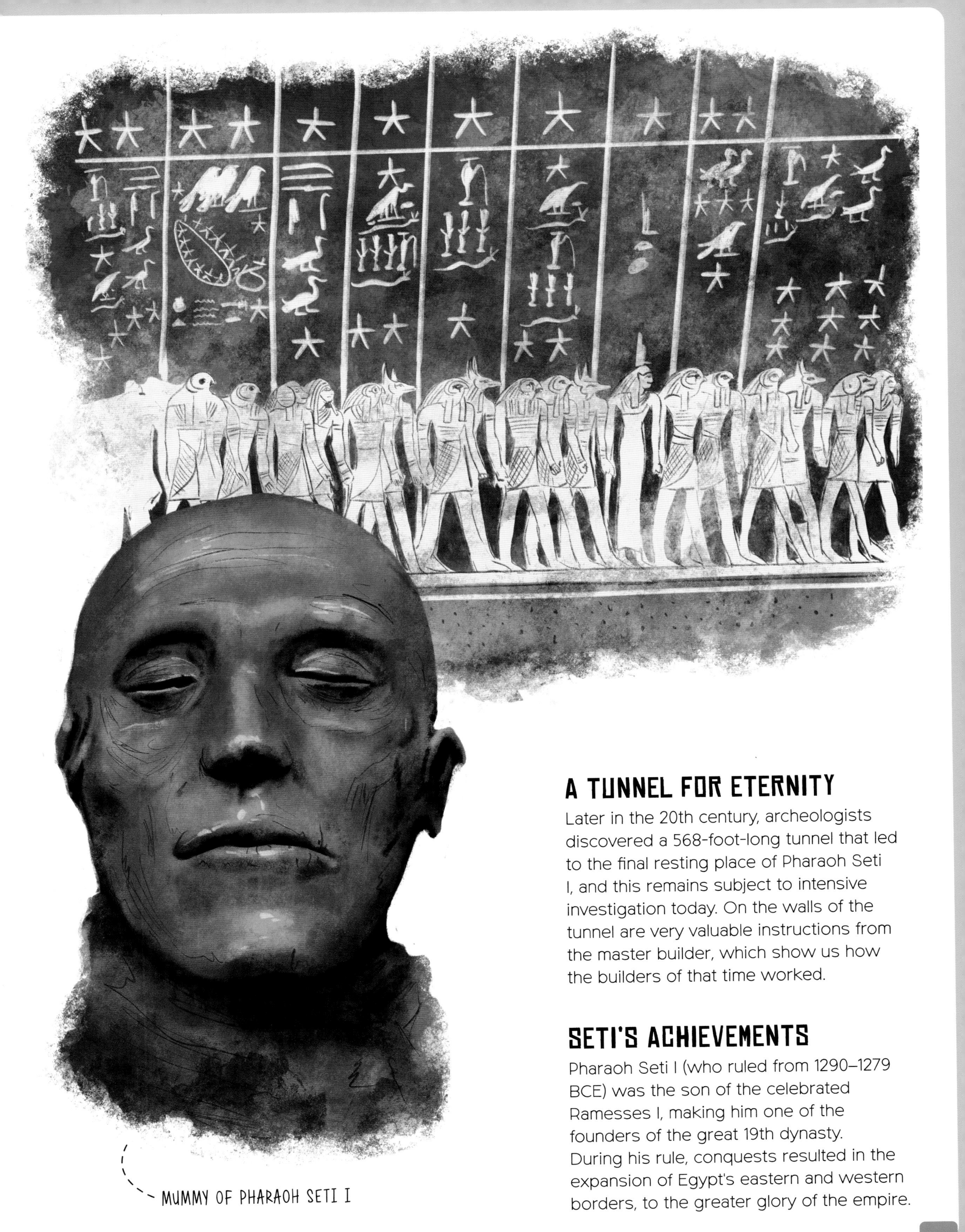

MUMMY OF PHARAOH SETI I

A TUNNEL FOR ETERNITY

Later in the 20th century, archeologists discovered a 568-foot-long tunnel that led to the final resting place of Pharaoh Seti I, and this remains subject to intensive investigation today. On the walls of the tunnel are very valuable instructions from the master builder, which show us how the builders of that time worked.

SETI'S ACHIEVEMENTS

Pharaoh Seti I (who ruled from 1290–1279 BCE) was the son of the celebrated Ramesses I, making him one of the founders of the great 19th dynasty. During his rule, conquests resulted in the expansion of Egypt's eastern and western borders, to the greater glory of the empire.

SUTTON HOO

(ʌtn ˈhuː)

DISCOVERED BY:
E. M. Pretty and archeologist Basil Brown

A VASTLY IMPORTANT DISCOVERY REVEALING LITTLE-KNOWN DETAILS ABOUT THE EARLY MIDDLE AGES IN BRITAIN.

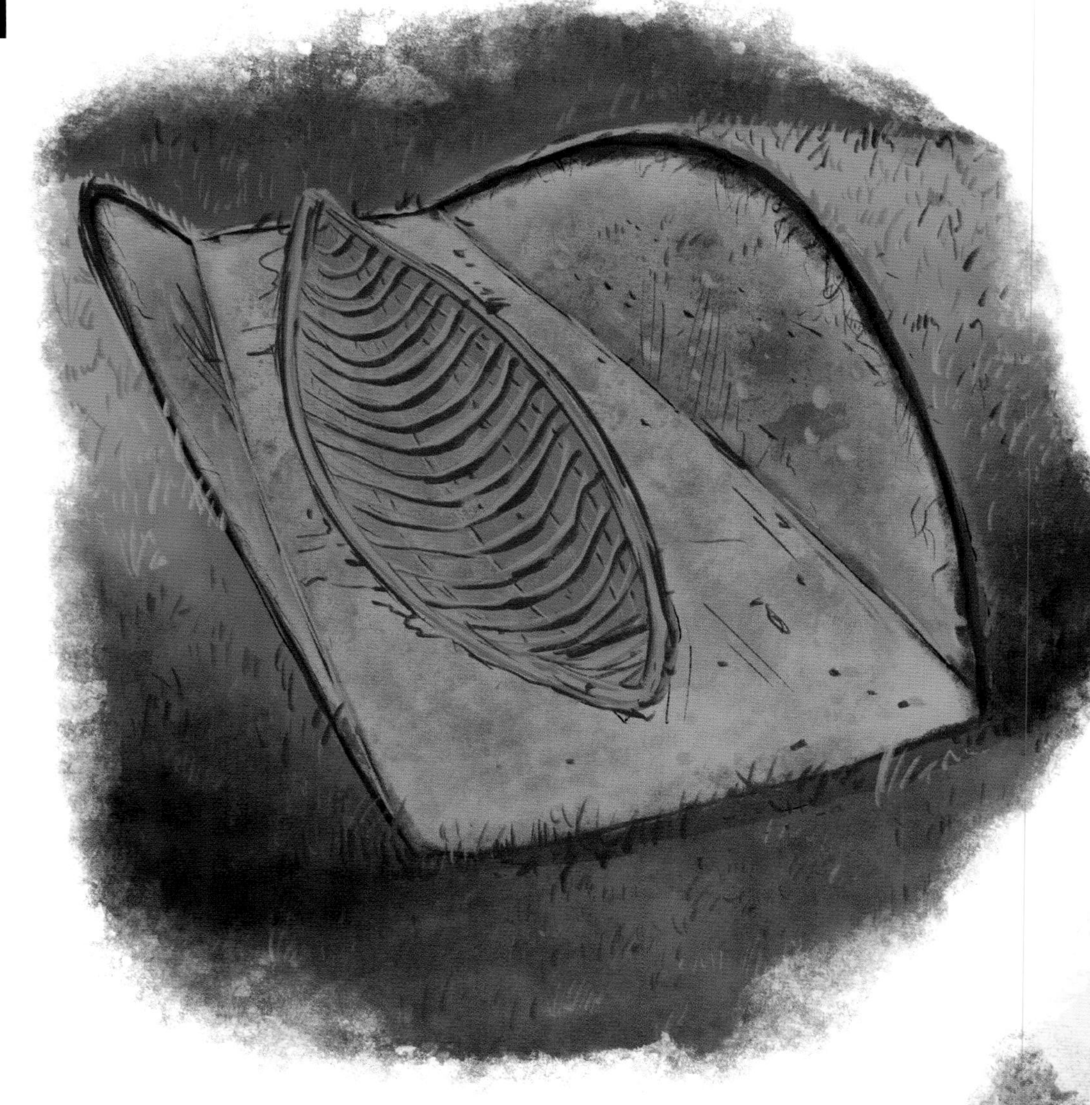

WHAT COULD BE IN THOSE HILLS?

Mrs. Edith Pretty was a wealthy Suffolk landowner. Since she had enlightened ideas, it was natural for her to ponder what was concealed by the obviously manmade hills on her estate. In 1937, she asked archeologist Basil Brown to research the area, which he did with pleasure and scholarly zeal.

SUCH BEAUTY!

Before long, Basil Brown had cause to rejoice: one of the mounds on Mrs. Pretty's land revealed the most spectacular early medieval tomb ever found in Europe in an undisturbed state. Dating from the 6th or early 7th century AD, it consisted of a burial chamber and AN 89-foot-long ship. Judging by the effort involved, the person interred here was surely very important. How exhausting it must have been to dig such a large grave! And imagine the work involved in felling the trees to build such a chamber and moving the great ship to dry land.

EQUIPPED FOR THE AFTERLIFE

In the burial chamber, Brown discovered many beautiful banqueting bowls, luxury hanging bowls, silver imported from Byzantium, precious cloths and fabrics adorned with gold, plus a ceremonial helmet with a human visage. Also found were leather boots and armor. But the tomb did not contain a body. It had either dissolved in the acidic soil or was interred elsewhere.

A TENT FOR THE DEAD

At the center of the ship was a wooden tent decorated with exquisitely woven tapestries. In this tent, the skeletons of two women were found on a bed. Scholars would later determine that the elder of the two died from cancer aged 70 or 80 and that the younger died at around 55. Both women ate mainly meat, so there is little doubt that they were Vikings of a higher social class. Viking commoners ate mainly fish.

VIKING QUEEN?

Scholars still don't know who the buried women were. One theory is that the elder woman was the Viking queen Asa, grandmother of Harald Fairhair, the first King of Norway. The younger woman may have been the slave of the elder, sacrificed after her mistress's death, in accordance with custom.

ESSENTIAL ITEMS

In addition to the remains of two women, the ship's hull contained gifts in the form of 15 horses, 6 dogs, 2 oxen, a decorated cart, 3 sleighs, valuable fabric, beds, and everyday items considered essential for the two women's journey into the afterlife. It is likely that many other gifts and objects were looted from the grave during the Middle Ages.

DISCOVERED BY:
Oskar Rom (a farmer)
and Professor Gustafson

DISCOVERED BY:
workers digging a well

TERRACOTTA ARMY

ONE OF THE MOST IMPORTANT HISTORICAL FINDS OF THE 20TH CENTURY.

FALLING INTO THE PAST

"We're falling! Help!" The well-diggers in the village of Xi'an must have been frightened on the day in 1974 when they fell into a large pit and found themselves staring into the eyes of a silent army of terracotta men. Their fear likely turned to astonishment as they discovered an army several thousand strong. The farmers in the village immediately called for the help of archeologist Zhao Kangmin.

ARMY OF IMMORTALS

This army of 8,000 had guarded the eternal rest of the first Emperor of China for two millennia. Each soldier is unique, with his own expression and stance, and even the lines on his palms differ. They are divided into companies by rank, including archers, charioteers, cavalry, and their commanders, all equipped with functional weapons and ready to defend against invaders at any time. The soldiers would have originally been painted to make them indistinguishable from real men. On average, each soldier is about 6 feet tall and weighs over 200 pounds. They even have horses and chariots.

WHERE:
China,
near the city
of Xi'an

WHEN:
1974

ONE OF 8,000
SOLDIER STATUES

A STATUE IN ITS
ORIGINAL FORM

THE EMPEROR'S SLEEP MUST NOT BE DISTURBED

The famous Terracotta Army is part of the magnificent tomb of Qin Shi Huang, the first Emperor of a united China. It was made by over 700,000 workers over 40 years. Because the tomb has a lot of traps to protect the Emperor's rest, scientists have not explored it completely yet.

EMPEROR AND UNIFIER

Emperor Qin Shi Huang ruled from 247–210 BCE. He unified the seven Chinese kingdoms. He ascended the throne aged only 13.

Scan the QR code for more
information and sources.

© B4U Publishing for Albatros, an imprint of Albatros Media Group, 2023
5. května 1746/22, Prague 4, Czech Republic
Written by Štěpánka Sekaninová and Tom Velčovský
Illustrations © Adam Wolf
Translated by Andrew Oakland
Edited by Scott Alexander Jones

Printed in China by Leo Paper Group

BLACK SEA SHIP
4th century BCE

TERRACOTTA ARMY
3rd century BCE

MŠECKÉ ŽEHROVICE HEAD
3rd century BCE

DEAD SEA SCROLLS
2nd century BCE – 1st century CE

VENUS DE MILO
2nd century BCE

SUTTON HOO
6th–7th century

CHICHEN ITZA
7th–16th century

OSEBERG VIKING BURIAL SHIP
9th century

4th century BCE

0

1st century